Becoming Myself

To David & Jean Bell,
with appreciation
for their friendship,

Mary

Becoming Myself

MY LIFE IN LETTERS AND VERSE

Mary E. B. Feagins

Mary Feagins

North Carolina Friends Historical Society
Greensboro, North Carolina

Published by:
North Carolina Friends Historical Society
P.O. Box 8502
Greensboro, North Carolina 27419-0502

All photos are from the author's collection.

Chapter Six: Alternative Service was published in a slightly different version in *The Southern Friend: Journal of the North Carolina Friends Historical Society,* Vol. XIV, No. 2 (Autumn 1992) and is reprinted with permission.
Excerpt from *Tending the Light* published with permission of Pendle Hill Publications.
Letter from David Madden published with permission of the author.

ISBN 0-942585-17-8
Library of Congress Catalog Card Number 00-109933

To the reader who finds enjoyment and meaning in my book,
and to all who have helped me define myself

CONTENTS

FOREWORD

Mary E. B. Feagins, author of *Tending the Light* and translator of Anna Sabine Halle's *Thoughts Are Free*, had poems published in the *Davidson Miscellany, Guilford Review, Quaker Life, Friends Journal,* and *Award Winning Poems of the North Carolina Poetry Society.* She taught German at Guilford College from 1956 until her retirement in 1982. She is the wife of Carroll S. Feagins Sr., Professor Emeritus, Philosophy, at Guilford. They have two married sons and a married granddaughter.

From early childhood, she was inclined to take seriously the Greek admonition "Know thyself"—and thy neighbor, too! After majoring in philosophy at Goucher College, she took her master's degree at Duke in the same field. Her travels abroad, which have been so influential in her writing, began with summer study in Heidelberg and a junior year in Munich at the time Hitler marched into Austria. Her private travel, often as a visiting Friend from New Garden Friends Meeting, has included Britain, most of Western Europe and parts of Eastern Europe, and Russia. In connection with the Guilford College study abroad program, she and her husband led summer sessions in East and West Germany from 1974 to 1982 and established a Munich semester program in 1978. They spent the 1965–66 year stationed in New Delhi participating in the Quaker Conferences and Seminars Program ranging from Afghanistan to the Philippines, with orientation in Japan and sessions in Nepal and Sri Lanka.

The present volume began some years ago as an autobiographical novel, "Becoming Herself," partly inspired by remarks of Colin Wilson in *The Outsider* (1956) lamenting the absence of a "Portrait of the Artist as a Young Woman." The encouragement of friends and readers eventually led the author to create a genuine autobiography, drawing on her extensive letters, journals, and poems to recreate a personal life influenced by the critical historical events and philosophical issues of the twentieth century. The work is rich in political, social, and psychological awareness, and leavened with a gallant sense of humor. Living Mary Feagins's life through this book will leave the reader wiser and more optimistic about the human spirit.

Ann Deagon
September 2000

ACKNOWLEDGMENTS

Without the help of some special persons, I would not have turned my novel "Becoming Herself," into this autobiography.

Louis Rubin, former editor of the Algonquin Press, Chapel Hill, North Carolina, read early versions at least twice before he convinced me that my work did not have the required "fictional thrust" for a novel.

Rebecca Mays, editor of Pendle Hill Publications, Wallingford, Pennsylvania, encouraged me in the direction of autobiography. Two Quakers, M. Gertrude Beal and Carole E. Treadway, librarian of the Friends Historical Collection at Guilford College, also led me to autobiography.

Carole, who has since become my editor, deserves my sincere thanks for her guidance in my reducing over four hundred pages of text to a better length without changing the essential wording of my story.

Last, yet first, I thank Carroll S. Feagins, Sr., my husband and closest friend, for being my sounding-board and patient proofreader.

1

EARLY BEGINNINGS

1917–1932

> tearing of membrane
> first spark of light in darkness
> flash flooding with a roaring in ears
> and then relentless counting my years

What is now known of my birth is only hearsay. It was difficult for all concerned, and it offended my mother, Sue, in two ways. Instead of arriving on her birthday as she had planned, I, Mary Ellen Brown, insisted on appearing a week earlier on the nineteenth of November, the birthday of the doctor. Furthermore, I caused uncontrolled hilarity that she could hear going on in the next room while waiting for her firstborn to be cleaned up and brought back to her. It seems that a birthmark in the small of my back resembled a flag, which the nurse considered an amusingly patriotic symbol for the year 1917.

All of my childhood history is, of course, partly hearsay. My memory shares a split screen with that of my mother, who said that I learned to sing while learning to talk:

> Smile a-while, I kiss you sad adoo,
> when the years woll by I come to you. . .
> so wait and pway each night fo' me
> til we meet again! . . .

I learned to read and to write as I learned to sing. My cousin,

Hope Willcutts, was the one who pointed out the connections between memorized Mother Goose rhymes and letters and syllables under the pictures. Later, after I had started to school, I spent hours making connections between words and sentences and the exciting pictures in the *National Geographic* magazine. By the second grade, I had written my first story, about a poor little boy who found and returned a wallet to a rich man who rewarded him magnificently. My father was so proud of this that he took my handiwork to his office in the Central High School building and had Miss Jane, his secretary, type the manuscript (almost a page long, single-spaced) and then mount it on blue construction paper. How pleased I was with my first "publication"! I kept it for many years, until when I put away childish things.

Muncie, Indiana, was not a bad birthplace. It had two green parks where we could play and have picnics. The public school system was advanced in comparison to those in the East and South. (My father, Glen, discovered this much later when our family moved from the Hoosier state to Baltimore, Maryland, where he would become the principal of Boys Occupational School No. 93.) There was an active YMCA with a good cafeteria, where the family could eat out often enough to give Mother a rest. There were, also, four distinct seasons of the year offering such recreational delights as swimming, roller-skating, sledding and baseball. These were my favorite sports, although Muncie was Hoosier-oriented to basketball.

My childhood was shared by my brother David, nineteen months younger, who was as blond as I was brown-haired. I remember learning to swim in a cold Michigan lake when I was three or four years old. My father expressed great pride over this accomplishment and I basked in his praises. This could have raised a permanent barrier between David and me—especially since I was a show-off in physical prowess. Nevertheless, I was eager to teach him all I knew and to protect him from physical assaults by bullying peers. It was only natural that I would be the one eventually to teach him to swim ten years later.

While Muncie was earning its title of "Middletown" as part of the first sociological study of an average Midwestern town, a sampling of families included ours. According to Mother, David's intelligence matched or, perhaps, surpassed, mine. When a young psychologist asked me to define a chair, while David waited out of earshot, I gave a simple definition "Well . . . a chair has four legs and a back and a seat to sit on."

David's response was prompt and clear. He looked at the lady with surprise, saying "Oh, anybody knows what a chair is. Look. There's one." He pointed to the nearest example and with that disdainfully returned to his toys. Mother sat in silence.

Sociological studies must be easier to conduct in countries where classes are more distinctly stratified. I recall my problems while making my own study after I had started to public school. I was an outgoing person and was interested in all my new companions. As far back as I can remember I was eager to classify myself and my family in relation to my schoolmates and their families. Since my friendships developed more by chance affinities than by design, I did not understand at all why my mother began to express concern about a few of my favorites. I soon learned that I could bring home anyone I wished for play. Nevertheless, Mother always made inquiries, by telephone if possible, and tried to meet at least one of the other parents before she permitted me to play with friends at their homes. I never became reconciled to the fact that one of my favorites lived "on the wrong side of the tracks"—whatever that meant—so that I could never go to her house.

I discovered through reading that there were advantages to being "rich." I overheard and later participated in many discussions concerning our family's lack of money for certain wants and needs. I learned the difference between "wants" and "needs" and felt secure that real needs would always be met with something left over for approved objects of desire. My education in choosing priorities advanced long before that word became part of my vocabulary. Still, in comparison with some of my friends whose families seemed to have more money than ours, I found myself doing and enjoying things that apparently were not available to others. I thought about this and finally asked, "Mother, are we really rich or poor?"

She looked into my brown eyes searching hers. "We are rich," she stated carefully, "in the things that money cannot buy." This reply satisfied me then and later took on more meaning as I gradually became aware of the varieties and inequities of existence.

I approached adulthood with an increasing understanding of the nature and potential of my body. I began the never-ending task of trying to master the art of balancing my control over it with its control over me. This balance was maintained by proper choices, where

I had freedom to choose, and by graceful acceptance and compliance, where no such freedom existed. The awakening of consciousness to this problem began early, with homely lessons drawn from my own private experiences as well as my mother's and, less directly, from my father's instruction. Seeds were sown that could develop into the grace needed for ordeals of "acceptance and compliance" accompanying my development into the female rather than the male person of my initial preference. I gave up reluctantly the dream of going to sea as a naval surgeon like my Uncle Mort.

My female cousins and I considered ourselves fortunate to share an unique aunt, whose headstrong ways provided entertaining and enlightening anecdotes for our mothers to use in admonishing us. There was, for example, the story of her as a girl hurling her hairbrush across the room as she declared firmly that she intended for her first monthly compliance with what seemed an unjust, exclusively feminine, experience to be the last one as well. My cousins and I saw immediately the futility of such childish behavior, especially since we knew first hand what a headstrong adult this aunt had become. Later, I realized that her anecdotal value should have made her my favorite aunt; it produced the opposite effect. In spite of the fascinating stories told about her and, later, her contagious devotion to teaching and preaching, she remained in our eyes the female person least to be emulated. By the time my cousins and I had reached that significant period of adolescence, we had found the necessary patience for yielding to our "natural" role.

My most cherished privilege from childhood was to escape the limits of time and place through reading. I could lift my eyes from a book and ponder at will—something that television was later not to permit because it would give no opportunity to resume concentration at the same place in the program where my fancy interrupted me. With eyes at rest, I was free to fantasize and my mind became filled with lands and inhabitants as real to me as those confined to time and place.

When I played "Heidi in the Alps" with Almajane Halbert, my school friend since the second grade, I felt an inner resolve to become a real Heidi, climbing the real Alps. It would be only a matter of time, I was certain. My mother had secured permission from Mrs. Kitzelman, whose property covered several suburban blocks nearby, for us to play on her estate. There we had "mountain" excursions on an outcropping of rocks and picnics of "goat cheese." An artificial pond became our "Alpine" lake where I taught David to swim. My mother's direct and simple intervention to help me realize a dream-world taught me that the line between fancy and fact could be crossed in either direction.

Before my parents started taking David and me to church, religion apparently played an important part in my life. Mother was a "staunch believer" and Father affirmed the hope that his children would find her faith, which he had been "born without" and was "still seeking." The Methodists had reclaimed Mother's mother when Grandmother Willcutts left the Quakers, whom she had joined to please her in-laws. Grandfather Willcutts, who was supposed to start attending Quaker meeting as his parents had hoped, never did reform, but stayed home to turn the vegetables around the roast in the oven. Gradually, Grandmother Willcutts began to miss the music and "livelier" services of her Irish forebears. That is how Mother grew up a Methodist with only vague memories of attending Quaker meetings.

So I began as a Methodist. I was impressed by the lessons of the Old and New Testaments, both of which I began to read rather early. I believed them to be of equal historical importance. I adopted, almost unconsciously, the idea that it was of enviable value to be "chosen" by birth to be a Jew, like my schoolmate, Marian Levin, and Jesus himself and then to be "converted" to some form of Christianity reflecting the life and teachings of Jesus. Still, another experience had more influence on my religious development than the church into which I happened to be born or any single set of scriptures. I have described it once before in a Pendle Hill pamphlet, *Tending the Light*.

> I was around five years old and was skipping barefoot up an alley behind our house. The day was sunny, the sky blue. I was filled with a sense of power, derived probably from my awareness of the pennies I had been given to spend on my favorite candies. This was, I believe, my first trip to the grocery store alone, and it was an excursion solely for pleasure. Suddenly I felt completely overwhelmed in a most wonderful way by the great expanse of universe around me. It was the first time I had felt this way. It was quite different from earlier feelings of the expanse and magnitude of the dark, which had evoked fear and loneliness as I lay in my bed at night and which had often prompted me to cry out for the comfort of my par-

ents' arms. I felt now the presence of a friendly observer watching over me with approval and encouragement. I sensed simultaneously that the approved freedom to venture, to search, and to choose was a source of great happiness, even though I am sure I could not have put this feeling into words. As I look back over my life, it was perhaps the only time I ever experienced such an overflowing feeling of joy in freedom without an accompanying sense of responsibility to others. There was an unforgettable awareness only of my independent self and of that detached friendly spirit around me.

Another early idea that I might have been chosen by birth to be a genius, was quickly corrected by a teacher who assured the entire class one day that there was not a genius among us. Although I appeared, at least to myself, to be very bright and felt some disappointment at her assertion, I soon became grateful to have less responsibility to the intellectual world. It was probably this teacher who introduced me to the *Testament of Youth*, by Vera Brittain, an author who was to be influential in turning me toward pacifism in spite of my natural tendency to exhibit a fiery temper.

Our family was inclined to very physical, even violent, expressions of feeling and will. These were usually verbal, but not always. All of us engaged in childish quarrels, including our parents between themselves. My father and I were often in conflict because he would not tolerate "impudence" and I insisted on speaking my mind when I disagreed with him even with the prospect of a carefully aimed slap at my offending mouth. Mother, who would have never allowed her husband to abuse her physically (and I never saw signs that he did), would get upset at these scenes. She herself would apply a small switch only to my brother David, who was as stubborn as I in his more devious actions but less apt to be outspoken, waiting for his mischief to be discovered. As far as I can remember, however, I was the only one who was disgraced, at age nine, by being sent to the school principal's office because of a public, hair-pulling, fist-wielding altercation with another child, Ladonna Carmichael. We became good friends after this, and neither of us could explain how we had ever fallen into our folly. We agreed only on one point: the other had "started it."

An especially refining influence came to bear on my feisty disposition. Although I would have preferred ballet, I endured piano lessons for several years. After every piano recital, at which I performed dutifully and usually without any mistakes but with little display of talent, I asked the persistent question: "Now may I get a library book?" I had free access to the family library, even to the large medical encyclopedia containing all the facts of life then available to the layperson. Perhaps my parents were wise to allow me to delve at will into this manual of health and disease and to become familiar with its colorful illustrations that excited awe, fear and sometimes even horror in me. I was never able to contemplate its mysterious diseases for long without a tinge of nausea. I came to believe that I knew all I needed to know on the subject of sex that demanded so much attention from my blossoming contemporaries. This book and the *National Geographic* inspired an early romantic interest in science and travel, further enhanced by the visits of Uncle Mort, who brought back stories and mementos from Europe and China. Romantic interests vied with serious questions in directing my reading tastes.

Reading and daydreaming led to an increased interest in writing. An inclination to "make believe" was closely related to an early need to share new ideas. The inspiration to create vehicles for these ideas in the shapes, sounds and rhythms of pleasing phrases came first from the exposure to nursery rhymes. I soon found that most of my own fantasies and compositions would vanish completely if I did not quickly put them onto paper.

As with most children, "making believe" took another form. I well remember my first attempt to make someone believe a "story." (Mother did not call it a lie.) I attempted to convince my mother that I had not disobeyed her admonishment not to touch the outdoor faucet when I finally confessed to having used lengths of tough grass to turn the handle so that my hands had not touched it. The grass had done it, I insisted. The memory of Mother's "lecture," patiently drawing distinctions between truth, falsehood and rationalization, never quite left her penitent daughter.

A large cherry tree in the backyard gave me a high perch for secluded reading and writing. I had wrapped around and woven ropes between forking branches of the tree and we climbed it often. Pitting cherries at canning time was one of my earliest childhood tasks, shared by David. I derived aesthetic pleasure from lying in the grass under a clear sky and peering through the transparent skins left after I carefully sucked out the sweet-sour pulp. The change in the shades of blue sky viewed through the pale pink skins gave me a special delight, which I shared with no one. It was an experience of beauty rivaling my perennial enjoyment of the cherry blossoms.

David and I were always seeking high perches. Climbing the trellis to the garage roof was frowned upon, but not so much as crawling out onto a dangerously accessible part of the house roof. Not even the explanation that we felt closer to Heaven up there removed the ban from this activity. The garage roof was also finally forbidden after David was caught just in time to prevent his jumping off with an umbrella as a parachute. He was caught only because I had told on him.

Perhaps our favorite activities were connected with winter snowfalls. Sledding and ice-skating sent us home with red cheeks and numbed toes that we remedied by sitting in front of the fireplace, toasting marshmallows and drinking hot chocolate. Mother made ice cream by spooning the purest deep snow from under its crystalline crust. Snow was the purest of all things, to my mind. One of the greatest pleasures was to lie down in it, sweep my arms up and down, and then to arise and look down on the angel pattern I had made.

The value of purity was engraved early in my mind. I could never forget an early lesson about this; but the simile, instead of snow, was clear, unpolluted water. The emotional impact of this imagery on the life of a child like me was considerable. From all external appearances, I was an ordinary little girl. Yet, a more than ordinary preoccupation with ideas, such as Good and Evil, Right and Wrong, Fairness and Unfairness, Life and Death, Beauty and Ugliness, set me apart from my friends. They enjoyed my participation in the usual games at school but grew impatient at my preference outside school for solitude spent with books, pencil and paper. Despite the time I had dedicated to reflection I was not quite prepared for the use made of imagery in the incident that follows. Or, perhaps, I was prepared, after all!

* * *

I remember walking very slowly home from school. How was I to phrase my "confession" for Mother? To ease my conscience completely, I would have to tell the story as closely to the truth as possible. There I had stood with Johnny and a couple of other friends. Recess was half over and we were resting from a game of baseball on the graveled playground. Gravel was good for marking the field, but not for sliding into home-plate. We often looked longingly at the small (too small) plot of luscious green carefully tended near the school building. An iron bar separated the cement walk and the playground from the grass. The bar provided fun to those like me, short and agile enough to turn somersaults over it when no monitors were around. The cool softness of the green was especially tempting, but that sign was always there: PLEASE KEEP OFF THE GRASS!

"Hey, Meb! I dare you to walk across the grass!" Johnny was using the nickname that I had invented from my initials. (I was beginning to hope not to be called by my double-name for the rest of my life. "Mary" or "Ellen" taken separately did not suit my parents at all.)

"Come on! I double-dare you!"

We saw the two teachers conversing on the porch. It was almost certain that they would see me. Still, foolhardily, I accepted the challenge, and the inevitable happened. They called me over and told me to go inside and report to my teacher what I had done. With the shrinking heart of a culprit, I walked into the front door and out the back. I leaned against the brick building and felt a mixture of humiliation and dread. Dealing with Miss Winters would not be easy. My feelings began to change slightly, however, when Almajane came to join me. The sympathy of this best friend was a great comfort. Shedding a few tears, I shared my righteous indignation that we could not walk on such a beautiful grass carpet with our tired feet burning inside scuffed shoes. Gradually, I convinced myself that the teachers who had scolded me would very likely forget the episode. When the bell rang for the rest of the morning's classes, the two of us crept meekly into Miss Winter's room and eagerly pulled books and pencils out of our desks. All seemed to be going well. Nothing was said before classes let out for noontime, and things went on as usual after I had returned from a quick lunch at home. Nevertheless, when time approached for afternoon recess, Miss Winters looked sternly down on me and said,

"You will remain inside with me."

A grave discussion followed, with me at my desk and a rather cramped Miss Winters folded into one in the next row.

"The sin of disobedience is not to be taken lightly. It can become a habit, as can all matters of sin. You not only disobeyed a rule, which you were quite able to read and to understand, but you then disobeyed the teachers who told you to report to me."

Miss Winters paused to note the effect that her sermon was having on her usually well behaved pupil. Since I was sitting there in a subdued silence, she went on, "What you have done has defiled your soul. Your sin of disobedience is like a drop of ink in a glass of water. The water is no longer pure, and every sin that follows will add to the impurity."

It was beyond my ability to keep to myself the obvious way to mend the situation. I spoke up eagerly: "But you can always pour out the dirty water and start over with a fresh, clean glass!"

Miss Winters looked quickly at my serious face turned toward hers. She could find no trace of impudence in its expression. She had no cause for further reprimanding. With a sigh of exasperation, she rose saying, "You may sit there and think over what I just told you. Sins cannot be erased as easily as you seem to think."

The vision of a soul getting blacker and blacker as it grew older could depress a seven-year-old, but not for long. I remembered the clear, cool water flowing into the bucket as I pumped from the deep well at Grandmother Brown's. I saw again how it sparkled in the many glasses distributed around the table where I was seated with my numerous uncles, aunts and cousins. Wells dug deeply enough— through layers of rock—neither went dry nor became easily polluted, Grandfather Brown had told me. Surely, I had no reason to accept Miss Winter's picture of reality. I would tell my mother the whole story. Knowing that she would frown on my behavior but believing in her forgiveness, especially when I had already done penance by the loss of recess, I put the matter out of my mind until time came for school dismissal. By then, I no longer had any fear of the vision of the contaminated soul. I need only think about how I would present the situation to Mother, receive her absolution and start afresh the next day.

Years would pass before a philosopher was to introduce me to the idea that some opposing values of equal importance cannot be pursued without the loss of one or the other. "Purity" is worthy of maintaining; "richness of experience" is equally worthy of attaining. I was to learn that I could never enjoy the latter without a comparable loss of the former. Lost innocence could never be restored.

* * *

Fortunately, not all the teachers in Emerson School were like Miss Winters. A beloved fourth grade teacher, young and pretty, encouraged me in my writing. She praised my short play, "The Quarrel of the Seasons," (the title may have been borrowed) and had the class put it on for our parents. As the author, I was allowed to choose the part of the Fairy Queen, who spoke her lines in prose and was the reconciler in a final speech given after Spring, Summer, Fall and Winter had each vied with the others as they recited their quatrains—of unusual merit, Mother told me proudly, for such a young poet. And how sweet she said I looked in the costume she had made for me!

My love for Miss Leslie was the first in a series of similar affairs. One, especially, involved Miss Jewett, a beautiful young woman just out of graduate school, who taught English and Latin during my three last years in Muncie. It was as absorbing as any love to follow, filling night hours with fervent recollections and contemplations of this adored image and with plans for acceptable, attention-getting strategies for the next day. The fact that I was physically a "late bloomer" caused me to feel left out of some conversations and activities engaged in by my more "developed" friends. I smugly asserted my intention to be "sweet sixteen and never been kissed" even as I envied the imagined experiences of my contemporaries. I felt wiser and better informed than they were (thanks to my mother and my wide reading), but I was pierced by an arrow of longing whenever my desires exceeded my freedom to express them.

This love, for one of my own kind, remained strong in me. One love blended into the next without my ever losing my loyal commitment to the first or feeling a loss in quality when, later, the objects were of the opposite sex. All along, through adolescence into adulthood, I was also expecting to find somewhere and somewhen a love that would encompass and surpass any of these. Such a love, I believed, would allow more satisfying, fully requited expressions of passion, and for it I was persuaded, by my mentors and by good judgment mingled with fear, to save most of my sexually maturing self.

Moving away from Muncie in 1932, before my fifteenth birthday, marked the end of my earliest "becomings." Sitting between David and our younger brother Joe in the back seat of the old Studebaker, I rode silently for many miles, staring through the windshield at the road ahead and the sky beyond. I sensed that I had left something very precious behind but was looking forward to something very exciting ahead.

2

BALTIMORE

1932–1937

A well-written life is almost as rare as a well-spent one.

The editor of our high school yearbook chose this quotation to place after the other notations beside my picture. I have never found its source, nor did I fully understand it at the time. I knew that it implied some appreciation for my love of writing. It was not until years later that I realized what significance my journal-keeping and letter-writing were to have for my life. I have much that is tangible and verifiable to jog my memory now as I recall the influences that shaped me. I see myself almost as a "third person," who is searching her sources, her own words from the past as they describe it.

* * *

I was lying awake listening to the noises of St. Paul Street. I was still getting used to the new sounds. Among them was the musical cry of the vendor, driving slowly by, enticing the neighborhood to buy his fresh vegetables. Without any written notes at all, I would remember his call forever:

Red ripe to-ma-toes, green beans, li-ma beans, sweet corn, ap-ples and po - ta-toes!

As long as it was summer vacation, I could spend a few precious moments in the morning remembering the Indiana home and friends left behind, with all the emotions that remembering evoked. It was better than lying awake at night. One of my teachers had once said, after I had told him of the enjoyment I derived from reflecting and planning before going to sleep each night: "You are going to regret this someday. If you don't want to become an insomniac, you'd better get out of this habit." Perhaps I could practice promptly falling asleep each night before school started in the fall.

My father had left our family in Indiana during part of the preceding year to accept his new position and to find a place for us to live. It was a temporary arrangement—far superior to what we had anticipated during those depression years. Colleagues of his were away for three months and were sub-renting their house to us. I was delighted to have this chance to live in one of the "row-houses" for which Baltimore was famous. Of course, neither Mother nor I would be scrubbing down the marble steps each morning as women in other areas of the city did. We were enjoying "playing house" in the neatly furnished rooms and watching traffic go by the deep bay window.

The location was suited to long walks down shady streets, lined with more trees than we had expected in the city. I liked to walk in one direction past the old Friends Meetinghouse on Charles Street. Mother had told me of the Quakers in her background—Willcutts, Marines, Clarks and others whose names I was to uncover much later. Also within walking distance was the Baltimore Museum of Art.

I discovered two things that summer. I loved strolling, almost daily, through the halls and side-rooms of the fine museum, as I gazed at the paintings and sculptures I had seen only in books. In the seventh grade, I had done a small bas-relief of the head of Mercury, felt appreciation for modeling clay, and marveled at the results of its firing. My attempts at painting had been less successful and I was determined to try my hand at this again, after more study. I found that I was actually missing the piano, which had been left temporarily behind with the rest of the stored furniture. I was beginning to appreciate much of the classical music that I had heard, although I lacked the talent to play it very well. There was no reason, however, for not trying to play some slow movements of favorite selections, as soon as the piano was again a part of our living room.

By the time school started in the fall, Dad had found a place to rent, on Dalrymple Avenue (later changed to Fairview), in Forest

Park. It was a duplex brick home shared by a German couple with one son about my age. On the other side, with a hedge between, lived a large family consisting of a widow with several sons and daughters, some old enough to have left home. Mrs. Glass, the mother, was friendly and announced to us as soon as she had welcomed us, "We're Catholics, but if you're Protestants, you ought to try the church on the corner across the street. Everyone says that Reverend McComb is the best pastor in the whole area."

That is how I became a Presbyterian. I joined the small, stone church with the rest of the family, by letter from the Methodist Church where I had been baptized. I joined, also, the large following of worshipers of the charismatic young bachelor. I remained a member throughout my years in Baltimore until my marriage there, even though I became more convinced weekly that I did not really belong.

Meanwhile, the Reverend McComb was called to a large church in New York City. I was left to engage in theological discussions with the local Presbyterian youth under another pastor. I could never accept their intolerance toward the attenders of the synagogue facing our church on another corner of Dalrymple Avenue or their smug assurance of their own "predestined" salvation. I seem to have been entirely unaware of my own intolerance toward the normal behavior of my youthful peers, who struggled with the inconsistencies between the Biblical ethics learned in Sunday School and their less than Puritanical behavior on Christian Endeavor picnics. I felt that they should be subject to the same demand I was trying to make on myself—to curb my sexual desires until the "right person" came along. This meant behaving in such a way as not to encourage advances from boys that I intended to spurn. If I agreed to a code of ethics and then behaved differently, I feared, I would be a hypocrite, one of those persons with whom churches are filled, according to my father!

I had the same feeling of difference between myself and the girls around me in high school. On occasion, during lunchtime, as I approached a table where a few friends might be giggling together, their chatter would stop. I gradually became aware that my presence was interfering with the good humor they found when they were telling off-color jokes. I remember my indignant protest at being referred to as "innocent" and my pointing out that it was better than being ignorant about the facts of life, which they seemed to be looking for in "disgusting" jokes. I suppose, I appeared to them as a somewhat arrogant prude.

In other respects, I fit in very well with my peers. This is illustrated by a rather remarkable thing that happened very soon after I had entered Western High School, once called Western Female Seminary. Baltimore had two or three public high schools for girls and others for boys, Polytechnic being the best known. (Forest Park, which David attended, was the only coeducational school then.) Upon inquiry, Dad had learned that Western had a superior academic rating and would admit into the tenth grade students who had completed the first year of high school under Muncie's new "6-3-3 plan." Furthermore, he hoped I would win one of several scholarships to Goucher College that were available to girls who graduated from Western. He advised me that It was the only way I could go to college since, with my two brothers to see through college, he could not afford to pay for me, too.

I did not question his reasoning at the time. Later, when I recognized its sexist unfairness, I rationalized that my father was just trying to spur me on to do my best and was confident of my success. For richness of experience, he could not have made a better choice of school for me, except for the lack of daily association with young men.

At the time of annual elections for class officers, one of my teachers suggested that I should not let my recent arrival keep me from running for office. Much to my surprise, I was elected sophomore president. I experienced popularity for the first time, in a class of over four hundred girls! I attributed much of my success to the Hoosier accent that had characterized my campaign speeches and seemed to intrigue my classmates. The formal business of presiding proved to be of great help in my effort to get rid of certain "mispronunciations" which had me at first asking for the "traysurer's" report and accepting favors with "playsure." A critical English teacher soon pointed out this problem with the "ea" diphthong. She also taught me to speak no longer about "bacon and aigs."

For two years, I continued to bask in my newly found popularity. I was given leading roles in two plays and one operetta. This astounded David, especially. He had never suspected a talent for singing in his sister. I was surprised myself. Only hard work and a good coach were to be thanked for my able solo performances. I was not surprised, however, that I was asked to take over the editing of the school paper. I was as happy as I could ever remember being at this chance to use my interest in writing. I also found myself surrounded by a substantial coterie of new friends and admirers.

Among these, I liked best a petite sprite with dark blonde hair, large gray eyes, generous mouth and boyish manners. Jean Lane became my most constant companion and rival, as Almajane had been at Emerson School. Jean also became the art editor of the paper. During our junior year, she was elected vice-president of the class and I was reelected president. During the campaign for senior class officers, we two friends put our friendship to the test by running vigorously against each other for the top office.

Every night, I sent up the same prayer: "You know, God, how much I want to win. I don't have to list the reasons why I deserve to be reelected. I've been a good president. It would be too bad to let a less experienced person take over the office. Besides, a victory in the coming election would make me the first person in Western High's history to serve three consecutive years as president."

Jean won. I was relegated to the vice-presidency. Nevertheless, I did not have to struggle very hard to be a "good sport" and to express some happiness for my friend's success. Indeed, as time went on, I looked back on this disappointment as extremely enriching. I had learned two lasting lessons. First, I learned that it was very foolish, for me at least, to put a lot of faith and energy in prayer for specific personal desires. So now I decided to adopt an eleventh commandment: Do not take the exercise of prayer in vain! Second, I learned that human beings can be fickle. My coterie of admirers transferred their affections overnight to Jean—so blatantly that the two of us had to laugh about it. Never again would I attach much importance to popularity.

Our friendship continued throughout our college years. We both won scholarships to Goucher, then still exclusively for girls. Our close companionship was disturbed somewhat by the fact that Jean chose to become a sorority sister while I declined for the reason that the same opportunity was not open to my Jewish friends. It is true, I knew of no one in particular who had been made unhappy by exclusivism among sororities; Jewish girls created their own sororities. And I know that Jean had never shown any anti-Semitism, which would be quite contrary to her generally friendly nature. However, since I had not had to confront racist or religious prejudice in my early years, I had become more sensitive to this issue as I became aware of it in Baltimore. I was shocked at expressions of anti-Semitism in this beautiful old city that I had grown to love in every other respect. Signs stating "Gentiles only" appeared at some public facilities. I overheard remarks claiming that the sale of property to Jews meant inevitably the decline of real-estate value and the eventual resale to Negroes. (The terms were all too often "kikes" and "niggers.")

I had friends with whom I liked to discuss differences between our respective religions. I even cherished the hope of converting a few to the Christian faith! My natural tact, however, made me careful to keep this hope secret. In addition, I had some reservations as to the superiority of one faith over another. That I had not been born into the exclusive race to which Jesus himself belonged was a source of regret for me throughout my early years. It was not until years later, when I read Dr. Zhivago, that I was presented with the idea that "exclusiveness" can lead to being "excluded." That helped to reaffirm a growing conviction that God, my Inner Voice to whom I had prayed and listened as long as I could remember, was accessible to every other human being who sought this Inner Companion—regardless of the name of the religion. As I gained an understanding of imagery and myth, I resisted accepting anything that smacked of dogmatism. I was developing, likewise, a healthy skepticism. It was not quite as strong as my father's; his skepticism, I noticed, was balanced by his faith in himself and in his family. He encouraged me in my search for knowledge in every way he could and was instrumental in getting me the financial assistance needed to supplement my scholarships.

He came home one evening with very exciting news. I was setting the table for supper when he appeared, somewhat breathless, for he had run up the long flight of steps leading to our house. "Guess what has happened! There is a very wealthy spinster in Baltimore who wants to meet you, one of two sisters who inherited a fortune from their father and eager to spend part of it helping others. The older one heard about you through one of my teachers. . . ." He went on to explain her interest in helping young women get a college degree so that they could be self-supporting. He had arranged for an interview.

The interview went well. A slightly plump, pleasant brunette of middle age received me in a simple but elegant apartment. Miss B. (she requested that I never reveal her name to anyone and I still feel bound to that) seemed to approve of me as I eagerly outlined my hopes for the future. She took me seriously when I promised to do my best to be worthy of any assistance she might give me. "All that I want in return," she told me, "is in the spirit of the movie *The Magnificent Obsession*; that is, someday, after you have finished college and have established yourself in your chosen field, I want you to help another as I am helping you, to see that the gift is passed along. . . . "

Feelings of pride and gratitude almost overwhelmed me as I left the apartment with the assurance that my benefactress would give me any necessary funds that I could not earn from scholarships or from my work in the Enoch Pratt Free Library, where I was employed under the National Youth Administration.

I do not like to give the impression that I was all seriousness and no fun. I was soon part of a "gang of girls"—several day-students without sorority sisters—who liked to lunch together, attend movies and concerts, occasionally, and who could be quite frivolous. As I've said, Jean and I were still good friends, although we saw less of each other. I remember one time at a concert, however, where the two of us went into an almost uncontrollable fit of giggles as we vigorously scratched our elbows to the rhythm of "The Flight of the Bumble Bee." I am sure this did not endear us to music-lovers around us. Yet, the academic life at Goucher meant for me, fundamentally, the continuation of a search for meaning in everyday experiences and gave me an exciting atmosphere in which to debate serious issues with those around me.

In fact, I told my first academic advisor about my fervent desire to major in philosophy. The young woman, an instructor in the Department of Chemistry, looked at me with an expression of determined disapproval and counseled me against majoring in anything before the end of my sophomore year. She encouraged subjects more "practical" than philosophy. But I was determined. I had found "Will Durant's *Story of Philosophy* in my family's library in Muncie, brought it with me, and read it over vacation during my first summer in Baltimore. If I had to wait to select a major, I intended to take as many courses in philosophy as I could in the meantime. And I did.

I had other ambitions, too, and later found it difficult to narrow myself to one area of study. I was still longing for some clear calling, some clear sign. If I could not be another Saint Joan or have a vision like Saint Paul's, or if I could not go to Annapolis and be commissioned for the Navy, perhaps I could follow in the footsteps of Marie Curie. Lines found in an old college notebook show a sincere interest in this direction but also reveal a persistent tendency to romanticize:

MY AMBITION

There is this that I would ask of my Creator
before my days upon this earth
are ended:
To have realized the value of true Science—
To have seen the glorious vision of her Spirit—
To have been inspired to follow in her footsteps—
To have seen the light of Truth she bears before her—
To have passed the Light to others
coming after.
This alone, it seems, would make my life worth living.

My interest in science accounts for my study of German. I had enjoyed the study of Latin since the seventh grade and French since the tenth. I was continuing with the latter and might have been content with the one foreign language if I had not seriously considered the pursuit of science, for which German was highly recommended. Little did I suspect that the study of that language would have a marked influence on my future, even though I never majored in it or in any other language. I never ceased to respect and have interest in the scientific search for truth. It soon became clear to me, however, that I definitely enjoyed the hours spent in libraries more than those spent in laboratories, whether biology, chemistry or physics. (I had tried all three.) My interest in science was more theoretical than practical, and I clearly lacked the patience and dexterity required for detailed operations, such as the use of chemical balances. I decided that I would be happier in the humanities and found the study of German so enriching in itself that I continued it throughout my formal education.

* * *

Dr. Goodloe, Professor of German, became one of the great influences in my life. She called me into her office one day and surprised me with news of a chance to study in Germany. She enthralled me with her description of a full-tuition scholarship for the University of Heidelberg for the coming summer. She pointed out how practical it would be for me to take advantage of being over there by staying for the Junior Year in Munich. She concluded by telling me that she had arranged for me to attend the next year and that it would not cost any more than a year at Goucher."

It took a little while for this to register in my mind. I had not quite seriously considered this particular dream, although I had entertained a few similar ones. Where was I to get the money? I reminded Dr. Goodloe, I could barely manage college expenses as it was. I lived at home and worked under the NYA and my dad couldn't possibly furnish the extra expense. He had my two brothers to think of. Then she reminded me of my benefactress, who "ought to have the chance to offer to help." I admitted it was tempting but I'd had too much given to me already. Her answer was ready and witty: "Them that has, gits."

I listened as she described the many exciting possibilities of a year abroad and continued to persuade me to let my benefactress know about the opportunity. I promised to talk it over with my parents and bring their opinions the next day.

Mother and Dad were as surprised as I had been. They eventually agreed with Dr. Goodloe, however, that I should at least tell Miss B. about it. So I made an appointment to see her.

If I had known, as I found out much later, that the summer scholarship amounted to a very small percentage of what the entire year would cost, I might never have presented the request. But Dr. Goodloe wisely (slyly) kept secret the value of the tuition fee for summer school in Heidelberg, and I could not hide my eagerness to take full advantage of the programs abroad. Miss B. did not keep me waiting long. She consented to pay for the trip and the year abroad, which should approximate the cost of tuition at Goucher but would include the additional expense of board and room since I could not be living at home.

* * *

The rest of the school year was jammed with plans for the summer and junior year. All this was in addition to preparing for and passing comprehensive examinations given at the end of the second year to decide whether a student should continue at the school. I expected to pass easily, and I did; but I was disappointed to receive only a slightly above average rating in every field except fine arts and literature, where I excelled. But it was understandable. I had been working in the fine arts department of the library and my love of reading had also "paid off."

The remaining months were highlighted, also, by my first "adult" romance. The same teacher in my father's school who had been responsible for introducing me to my benefactress had performed another service. She had arranged to have her nephew, Charles, accompany her and for me to accompany my parents to a school dance. That is how I met this rather handsome Johns Hopkins pre-med student, a couple of years older than myself. And that is how I had someone to ask to my high school prom. Attending both a high school and a college for girls had lessened my chances to meet eligible dates. Besides, I had not particularly missed this aspect of social life. I had enjoyed, rather, the small group of girls with whom I had lunched either in the City Girls Center or in a local drugstore. I had a favorite in the group, Louise ("Bert") Brandau, who attracted me both physically and intellectually and satisfied my need for someone special with whom to share affection and good-humored arguments. Then Charles began to pay me attention.

He was not the only young man I had dated, but the only one whose company I really enjoyed. (The boy next door had become a good friend but he was more nearly the age of David.) Charles was a very good dancer. He also liked horseback riding and drove me to York, Pennsylvania, a few times, where there were stables with horses to rent at a price affordable to students. Our dates were infrequent because Charles was a poor pre-med student, who earned his dating money by selling his blood! He was healthy enough to manage this as often as allowed. He was good-looking with his dark hair and eyes, and he had a wonderful sense of humor. The two of us had great fun, not the least of which was friendly arguing. Our points of view were quite different in some ways—especially when it came to philosophical concepts. We enjoyed the same activities but the fact that Aldous Huxley was his favorite author and Robert Browning mine is an indication of how opposing ideas might feed many fiery discussions. This made Charles all the more attractive to me and it is not surprising that he would be the one to give me my first kiss.

The first kiss, somewhat less than perfect because of the preceding hamburger with onions which I had not shared, led to others, more moving. By the time I left for my year away, I was convinced that I was falling in love. This became even clearer to me when Charles drove me, with Mother and his aunt, to New York City to see me off on the SS *Deutschland*. While we waited for the midnight departure he drove us to Central Park, where he invited me to get out of the car, leaving the two women alone for a few minutes while he gave me his last, lingering kiss. We both promised to write and looked forward to our reunion a year hence.

3

A JUNIOR YEAR IN MUNICH

1937–1938

Letting me leave home for a year in a strange land, I was to learn, was more difficult for Mother and Dad than I realized at the time. What they had been reading in newspapers and magazines about Germany under the Nazi regime did not make the prospect of separation any easier. Long talks with Dr. Goodloe emphasized the cultural opportunities and reassured them of the safety and careful supervision of the two academic groups of which I would be a part. Reluctantly, my parents entered into the planning with as much enthusiasm as they could muster. Mother was so little interested in my packing for the year that she gave me permission to go through her wardrobe and choose what I thought I might need to supplement my clothes. (She was my size exactly and always liked to shop for me and to share what she bought for herself.) She did not bother even to check the final results of my packing!

Mother went with me to the harbor and just before I boarded the ship, she slipped a note from Dad into my handbag.

June 18, 1937

My own darling daughter:

My heart is too full to tell you anything of the way I feel about your leaving us for a long year. But please don't worry or be in the least homesick ever.

Make new friends slowly and treasure the ones worthy of your esteem.

You are an unusual character, my dearie. I am more proud of you than anyone could possibly know. I love you, dear. Please forgive all my uncontrolled actions toward you and know always that you could mean no more to anyone than to

Dad

God bless and keep you safe for us. Auf Wiedersehen.

As I read the note, a deep surge of filial affection welled up within me, subduing the almost unbearable burst of spirit aroused by the excitement of departure. For a moment, alone in the crowd on the deck, I realized what I was leaving behind. My father's words evoked many memories of the love-hate relationship that had been ours. He had no more been able to restrain his hand from slapping me across my mouth than I had been able to repress the defiant words that I knew would anger him. We had never been able to disagree in silence, never been able to withdraw quietly before an oncoming argument. The note expressed poignant feelings that he had usually kept to himself. It also explains the unusual amount of personal detail that I was to share in future correspondence. Like Dad, I have tended to express feelings about close personal relationships best in writing.

Mother had gradually become more like an older sister in whom I still felt compelled to confide but with whom gradually I had found it easier to differ. Now, the first time away from my parents, I felt very briefly the infinite space and loneliness of independence. Then, almost instantaneously, I felt confident, ready for adventure and for the new responsibilities that I hoped to meet and fulfill well. I knew that the Inner Companion would always be waiting and ready when sought. With this, I joined the others who were leaving the deck to go to their cabins.

* * *

On this trip, I formed a habit that I have retained throughout my life: writing faithful descriptions of my adventures in my letters home. Nothing was remarkable in that, but what I did not anticipate was that Mother would keep all of these until my return. I am grateful for this because I can use them now to show that, in spite of my obvious joy in my new friendships and numerous German cultural opportunities, I was also experiencing a deepening concern for views encountered under Nazi influences. Other students like me were trying to be perceptive in the midst of subtle and not so subtle propaganda both in Germany and in news from the USA.

As I read again my letters from the ship, I can still feel the longing I had for my parents and brothers to be there with me. And I smile at my exuberance. My first postscript reveals my intention to get the most out of every moment aboard: "I haven't done one bit of reading! And I'm not being too reserved. But you needn't worry. I'm not being rash!"

Instead of reading, I spent spare time writing home. I numbered the letters, to be mailed in Ireland. As their contents show, I took advantage of all that life on board had to offer. I was a bit censorious of some "young Americans (not Germans)" who drank too much beer. I suspected they were showing off and admitted they could be rather "hilarious." I intended not to drink beer until we landed. I notice that I wrote in one letter, "I was a wee bit homesick last night because for a minute I didn't seem to fit but today that's gone." Perhaps my moment of loneliness is not hard to understand when I also wrote elsewhere, "Last night was the Bock Bier Fest. I went and had a grand time without drinking any beer"—hardly the way to fit in!

Everything was "absolutely perfect," including meals at 8:30, 10:30, 1:00, 3:30, and optional buffets at 11:00. There were dances, the usual games, and swims on top deck in a pool resembling a "large pigpen lined with canvas." We enjoyed excursions into tourist and first classes but decided, after one dance in first class, that third was "more fun" and our crowd "as good if not better." The best part of the ocean crossing was meeting people and practicing German with a variety of natives.

By July 7, 1937, I was sending my letters from the Pension Hornbeck, Blumenstrasse 4, Heidelberg. My arrival was somewhat unorthodox. I had studied my Baedecker guidebook with its detailed maps of cities and figured out the shortest route to Blumenstrasse. So, when my train arrived, I took a shortcut and inadvertently missed the place in the station where I was supposed to have my ticket collected. I missed Luisa, the maid, who had come to meet me and to carry my suitcase. Half dragging it through the gate of a high brick wall surrounding the pension, I climbed the steps to an imposing house of the same yellow brick and rang the bell.

A portly man with slightly bulging eyes, an equally bulging belly and a balding head opened the door. A Nazi button decorated his lapel. Herr Nassauer's smile was friendly but his voice was cool as he introduced himself and led me to the parlor, where his mother was waiting. Frau Nassauer's portliness was less clearly defined than her son's. Covered by a cloud-like voile frock, she blended into the armchair whose frame molded her plump figure into its shape. Her voice was cheerful as she asked me to take a seat and sent the maid for refreshments. As we waited I began to explain how I had left the station by a side street and had taken a more direct route to Blumenstrasse. Herr Nassauer interrupted my story to say, "Let me see your ticket." Chuckling, he called attention to the fact that the portion of the ticket from Darmstadt to Heidelberg was still valid. "You can ride a bike up there, spend the night, see the castle and two fine museums and take the train back, checking your bike in the baggage car—all for around six marks!"

I did take the bike trip to Darmstadt. Rachel, one of the two other Goucher girls, went along. Starting out at 1:30, we rode the fifty-seven kilometers (thirty-five and one half miles) in around six hours. Rain forced us to spend part of the time in a cowshed. We spent the day viewing Darmstadt. My only other expense was 40 pfennig (10 cents!) for checking my bike on the train."

My letters are filled with descriptions of life in the pension, of other boarders, many of whom were Italians, the food, bike trips into the Neckar Valley and my progress in German. "Any one who speaks English in our pension is fined 5 pf.! Also the Italians can't speak Italian, etc. . . . It's very important for us three girls to stick by the 5 pf. fine, for we share one big room. Our awkward attempts to speak German when we are in a hurry sometimes makes us break into fits of laughter. And we don't confide in each other as much as we would in English. We can't afford the price!"

At the Auslaenders Club dances I met Frenchmen, Italians, Greeks, Hungarians and Englishmen—all speaking English. Anna Ceresa, who lived in Pension Horneck with us, read and spoke German better than I did and helped me in our advanced literature class. She and her brother Alberto, I wrote, were "two of the most refined young people that I ever expect to meet."

I was quick to report my first impressions: "It is so interesting making friends from all over the world. It makes one stop and think just how insignificant we really are, after all. I'm afraid I never appreciated the importance of people from other lands before I left America."

I enclosed snapshots.

The pretty girl in the apron in the group of four is Luisa, the maid about whom I spoke. She is a darling, as you can see by the picture, and, as I said, she certainly can cook. I have gained weight since I've been here and feel fine—all because I eat more than I've ever eaten since the days I spent at Camp Sing-a-long. . . . We have now five Italians, including Marga's brother, Tonino. He is 24, a medical student like Charles and reminds me of him. He has a wonderful personality and I have a grand time whenever I go out with him—but we must speak a mixture of French and German mostly and sometimes a little Italian (which I'm picking up on the side) before we understand each other, since he speaks very little German.

A few words about Herr Nassauer. He is an enigma to me—so proper and polite in his manners toward us, but thoughtless and rude in some of his remarks at table. There are always several boarders for dinner and, sometimes, we are joined by a couple of elderly women. We've been told little about them except for the fact that they are paying guests who share a room above us, where they can have their meals alone if they wish. They remain to themselves most of the time. Herr Nassauer confided early to us that they were Jewish. Then he proceeded to make some slurring comments about Jews, in general. Although the two women were not present, I was afraid they could hear him if their door happened to be open as was the door to the dining room. I spoke up quietly but distinctly for his ears: 'How can you talk this way when you are receiving money from the two ladies upstairs?' He only laughed and said something about exceptions proving the rule. He is the only one I've met who boasts of being a member of the Nazi party.

By August 9, I was writing: "I had a wonderful time in Koblenz. . . . We got back at 8:30, in time for a date with Tonino . . . And now that I've mentioned Tonino, I can't stop there; for he is absolutely the most fascinating boy I have ever met in my life and I am more than fond of him. I didn't realize how much I liked him till I went away for the weekend; and now I know how I'll hate to leave this coming Tuesday. I guess it's just as well I'm going now; for I've been with him every day since he came (two weeks ago tomorrow) and we like each other better all the time."

I wrote of plans to correspond and hopes of visiting Anna, who had invited me to visit her in Italy. "But you needn't worry. I'm prepared to 'get over it' and forget everything if necessary. Tonino and I understand each other perfectly, regardless of the fact we must speak in French and German, and we realize the odds that are against us. He is almost 24, Charles's age, also a medical student, and from a well-to-do family . . . He has as many years of studying ahead of him as I have, if not more, and we both realize that a lot can happen in the meantime. But we have promised always to be very straightforward in our correspondence and if and when we see no hopes of a future of us together, we'll say so."

I expressed regret at not having Mother with me to confide in and went on. "It's hard to write all this in a letter, but I think you know me well enough to trust my common sense. I can't be sure yet whether I really love him or not, but I do know I've never felt this way before (even over Charles—much as I like him!). Anyway, I'm just the way I always was in my actions if not in my sentiments and thoughts. . . . By the time you read this I shall be well on my way to Munich and perhaps recovering from my sudden attack; so don't trouble your head about it any."

I learned an important lesson from my Heidelberg letter-writing and from the first few letters in Munich. I found out that replies to these confidences took so long returning that I often found myself in distress because my parents worried about matters that had long since settled down in my own mind and were no longer causing me any turmoil of spirit. Their expressions of sympathy, no longer especially needed, or comments revealing concern over problems already solved, or gentle chidings about what appeared to be intemperate drinking began to make clear to me that it was much better not to write anything that could be misunderstood or magnified in importance by distance. I remember that I laughingly said one day to a junior-year friend, "It did not occur to me that mentioning every glass of wine or mug of beer I drank, just because this was still a novelty for me, might leave the impression that drinking was all I was doing!"

My father became sufficiently alarmed about my infatuation with Tonino to say that perhaps I should not plan a trip to Italy. It took an exchange of several letters before the summer romance fell into proper perspective. I remembered, but did not share my recollection then, that I had become emotionally involved so quickly because I was hurt when Charles had taken so long to write. The first time I had allowed Tonino to kiss me (not counting the exciting kisses on my hand!) I actually made a mental statement that it would serve Charles right if I fell in love with someone else. Had not Charles himself advised me to be a little less reserved and more expressive of my emotions with others besides himself—but to be careful! He had been like the older brother I did not have.

I appreciated his counsel, for it was not long before I had to convince Tonino that not all American girls were free with their affections just because they were allowed to date unchaperoned. At first, this was not easy to do: Both Anna and Tonino had been surprised at my willingness to speak frankly on the subject of sex, which, according to Anna, nice Italian girls waited to learn from their husbands. He had assumed that my knowledge came from my own rather than vicarious experience. Even after my careful delineation of what I considered proper between unmarried couples, I had found it sometimes necessary to replace his arm around my waist when it began to wander elsewhere. I did not subscribe to the motto: anything goes so long as it's above the waist. But I saw no harm in moderately passionate kisses and looked forward to lingering goodnights on the landing of the stairway to the second floor, where the girls and I shared our room near the Italians.

After all was over, I could say that my demonstrations of love had been mostly verbal and my emotions had been expressed physically, almost entirely, in the most exciting dancing that I had ever engaged in. Tonino had taught me to tango and could lead me in Viennese waltzes better than any German I had danced with. What I did not know at the time was that I would never again find dancing so enchanting as it was in his arms.

In my desire to share as much as I could with my family without causing them unnecessary worry I continued to make my letters long and effusive. I had learned enough of a lesson, however, to cause me to leave the account of a later romance in Munich to share after I got home.

One of my early letters indicated that the political scene concerned me. I had recently received two letters from Jean and, at last, a very nice letter from Charles. Charles's letter had been opened for inspection. Herr Nassauer said we could write anything we liked and nothing would be done about it, that the officials were just looking to see if money was being sent out. I did not see why they opened incoming letters, though! "But it doesn't matter," I wrote. "All the talk I heard before coming over certainly was exaggerated. German people seem to be no more upset over affairs than the Americans who rave over politics there. In fact, not so much. And we have a pretty good opportunity to observe on our own account. I will have lots to tell you when I come home as you can imagine. But right now I can tell you that Germany is an ideal place to visit."

When I went through my letters years later, I became aware of the influences that changes of location, conversations with varieties of people and passage of time had on my opinions.

* * *

turning twenty in a time of turmoil
vivid encounters to haunt the heart
to challenge the remembering mind
at last to be recounted here

MUNICH VIA LEIPZIG

I was happy to have Rachel as companion on the trip to Leipzig. She was eager to see everything, had a sunny disposition and seemed never to tire of chatting with travelers on the train. We had brought along our bikes, which we retrieved from the baggage car at every stop and used to ride to hotels and then to tour the cities, often on rough cobblestones. In that fashion we managed to visit all the historical spots recommended by Miss Goodloe, who had arranged this additional cultural tour as a special gift to me.

In Leipzig, at last, I caught sight of my "beloved Professorin" Miss Goodloe, waving to us on the platform. I ran to greet her with a warm embrace. She told us that she had rooms for us at a nearby Hospiz where Betty Hall, who was returning to Goucher from her Junior Year, was waiting for us. The four of us had dinner at Faust's Auerbachs Keller. There we drank toasts—to the Past, Betty, having completed her year in Germany; to the Present, Rachel, enjoying the rest of the summer there but on her way home; and to the Future, myself, who would remain for my Junior Year. It was also apparent that Miss Goodloe, aware of my upbringing in a home without alcoholic beverages, wanted to use toasting as an opportunity to say a few extracurricular words about the proper way to drink socially and how to decline politely without offending.

The reunion with my teacher was most welcome, lovesick as I was. At our first private moment I let loose all the pent-up emotions and details that could not be shared in correspondence and found a comforting shoulder to receive my copious tears. I showed her a framed picture of Tonino that he had given me on the night of my departure and told her all about him. Her words of encouragement, along with a letter from Mother, returned me to the happy frame of mind of Heidelberg days.

In the next five days, Miss Goodloe introduced us to the great Leipzig library and to the home of Dr. Stumme, who had a famous Faust collection of everything he could acquire on the subject in art, music and literature. We had almost a week together in this city of culture and beautiful treasures: I planned to return. Who would have predicted that, before my return, this city was destined to become a part of the Eastern zone of a divided Germany?

LETTERS FROM BAVARIA

A letter dated August 27 reports that I was settled in Munich. At my first glimpse of the beautiful city I felt I could not compare it to Heidelberg. It was so much larger and probably would prove less romantic. But I hoped eventually "to love it as much as Heidelberg, probably for quite different reasons." I liked my accommodations and Frau Lüttgens, my *Hausmutter*, very much. I was allowed two or three baths a week, and the meals were "well balanced and very good." All this I received for 150 Marks per month.

Best of all, Frau Lüttgens would be leaving in September to visit a friend in Reisach bei Oberaudorf near a lake in the Bavarian Alps on the Austrian border. She would take me along. Instead of paying her, I was to pay her friend 4.20 M a day, cheaper than staying in Munich. It would be quiet there and the climate beautiful; so I would get a good rest—needed after my rather strenuous travels and before school opened October fourth.

I had been a little surprised after arriving in Bavaria to note the change in the customary greeting. In Heidelberg and Leipzig, I had heard "Heil Hitler!" everywhere. It was the only greeting. In Munich, the greeting was "Gruess' Gott!" Frau Lüttgens had told me this when I arrived but I soon found out for myself. There was a place near the Feldherrn Halle where there was an eternal watch and everyone was supposed to salute and say "Heil Hitler!" but that place could be avoided by taking a right fork and an alleyway. They called it "Druckeberger Strasse" (Shirker's Street). Most people took that way, I heard. They were hissed if they walked by without paying respect to where Hitler was nearly killed in his first, unsuccessful Putsch. I did walk by once, across the street and without even looking at the guard, and he hissed me.

Frau L. had an interesting dinner table, which would grow after University classes started and the other juniors arrived. Two were to ride with me to Reisach: Catlin Whitehead was from Anderson, Indiana, a Hoosier like me. Frau L. considered him a "typical American." I was never sure what that meant. I wrote home my first impression that Caitlin was "very nice, rather like our neighbor Hal but more intelligent and of a rather higher caliber . . . the type that makes a good pal." The other was a student at Oxford, William Dyfri Rees. He was Welsh and his middle name pronounced something like "Duffrie" although he allowed us to call him Bill. I was sure that Mother would like him best because he was "a real musician" and "played the piano divinely."

Another constant table companion, Herr Blumtritt, was not rooming with Frau L. It was his wife we would be visiting. She had moved to Reisach because she did not approve of her husband's hearty acceptance of Nazism. She supported herself and their sixteen-year-old son Eberhard by taking in paying guests. Herr Blumtritt had remained in Munich, where he owned a bookstore. Conversations at Frau L's table were often quoted in my Munich letters home. There we had freedom to speak on many subjects, including political.

One bit of advice, however, that the Millers, leaders of the Junior Year, gave us guided my own inclination to express my opinions freely. It was "to make our own observations, at the same time withholding our opinions until we had firm backing for them, and then approve or disapprove at will—but know why we think as we do." I reported then that I had seen and heard much of what, in some cases, I was "inclined to approve for Germany and in many cases, not—especially the propaganda sheet, *Der Stürmer.*" I did not forget that I was a guest—and a very well treated one—in Deutschland and, like a guest in a family, I intended to respect the ways of those around me. That was not hard to do because of the German people themselves. Most of those that I met were really likeable.

In Reisach, I met some of the most likeable. Frau Blumtritt, I wrote, was "a dear." I continued to describe some "interesting vacationers" there: "some young Germans and two Quaker ladies, one English and one German. I was quite attracted to a young German couple around my age. His name is Walter Kowitz who was on military leave. He was quite handsome—sort of a typical Siegfried, blonde hair and blue eyes. She was one of the prettiest girls I had ever seen, with dark hair and eyes, a flawless complexion and a smile that was always flickering across her face. He called her "Aennchen." (The name is short for "Anna" and sounds much prettier than it looks—something like "Entchen.") They were very much engrossed in each other, but they always had a friendly greeting for me and at supper exchanged reports of whatever excursions they had made during the day.

Spending these happy weeks in the Bavarian Alps provided an unforgettable interlude between two contrasting university experiences. I had taken advantage of the chance to improve my German and had taken seriously Eberhard's criticism of my pronunciation of the long "o" and of vowels in general. I was not nearly as fluent as Dyfri but less timid. Catlin was still struggling as a beginner with no formal instruction. I had become very comfortable in their company, although we all tended to be rather quiet in the presence of others. At the dinner table, the three of us were dubbed "Trappists" by Eberhard, as he good-naturedly explained the allusion to this order of monks with their vow of silence.

When time came to leave this idyllic setting, I followed quite naturally the German custom of writing a "poem" to celebrate such occasions and added it to the Blumtritt guest book along with quick sketches of three Trappists on bicycles.

Sommersprossen auf der Nase,	Summer-freckles on the nose,
Auf dem Fuss 'ne grosse Blase,	Blisters on the heels and toes,
Zunge mued' vom Redefluss	Tongue tired out from language flow
Fortlaufend von dem Morgengruss	Incessant from the dawn's hello
Bis Abends, doch des unerkannt,	Till ev'ning, still ignoring this,
Hat jemand mich "Trappist" genannt!	They call me "Trappist, quiet Miss"!
Ein Mondgesicht viel, viel zu rund	A moon-face that is much too round
Von manchem zugenomm'nen Pfund—	From many an easily added pound—
In solchem Zustand geh' ich fort	In such a state I go away

Von diesem wunderschoenen Ort.	From Paradise where I would stay.
Es tut mir wirklich leid zu gehen!	It makes me really sad to go;
Jedoch es gibt ein Wiedersehen!	Yet, I'll be coming back, I know!

—Reisach, September 1937

OCTOBER 2, 1937

When I came back to Kaulbachstrasse, Frau Lüttgens, who had come ahead, had everything fixed up for me. There were flowers in my room, a good supper was waiting, and there was a letter from Mother. I went to bed early that night, for I was tired. I had checked my bike through to Munich and left Oberaudorf at 5:06 P.M. I changed trains in Rosenheim and arrived in Munich at 7:30. That was my first train ride alone in Germany and it was lots of fun. In the station at Rosenheim, one of the railroad agents took me for an Italian. No one in Europe thought I looked like an American. I was always taken for Italian, French, Hungarian or the like. I thought it was because I did not wear makeup (indicative of Americans) and had the features of some Latins.

* * *

Shortly afterwards, more of the juniors arrived from America. They were friendly and jolly, yet seemed to take their work seriously. I was surprised to see that none of the three girls besides Mary and me wore makeup, either. It seemed that everyone had become temporarily a good German.

My early observations of conditions in Germany did not bear out what I considered to be the exaggerated impressions held by most Americans. The people appeared, in most cases, to be happy and contented under the Third Reich. But I observed in Germany as well as in America that although there was plenty of propaganda, it was so obviously propaganda that no one could fail but recognize it as such. In fact, I doubted that the subtlety necessary to make propaganda successful existed to as great a degree in Germany as, perhaps, in our own country. And I know absolutely one thing. The talk about Germans not being allowed to make critical remarks over politics seemed to be exaggerated. There were many people who were not National Socialists. And they expressed themselves without the consequences that were often pictured for them. There was in Munich a popular beer-hall entertainer who was well known for his political jokes. I considered the preference given to Nazis over anti-Nazis to be natural. It is common for the political party in power to give preference to its members, although I did not approve of the practice. I concluded that regardless of the difficulties Germany was going through, it still had many cultural advantages to offer.

* * *

I have a program among my papers that is dated April 17, 1988 and is headed: "YOM HaSHOA," Guilford County Holocaust Commemoration, First Presbyterian Church, Greensboro, North Carolina. For this occasion I was billed as "Retired Professor, Guilford College. Christian student in Nazi Germany at time of Holocaust." In my introductory remarks I said the following:

> This is the first time in my life that I have been on a program where I am billed as a Christian. There are so many kinds of Christians, so many with whom I do not feel comfortable, that I am sometimes reluctant to be labeled one. Yet I was born to a Methodist mother and an ex-Baptist father, was married in a Presbyterian church to which I belonged, was married by my husband's father, a Baptist minister, and I am now a member of a religious society that has its roots in Christian tradition—the Society of Friends called Quakers.

My contribution to the program was the reading, with comments of pertinent excerpts from the letters which form an important part of my story. Remember that they were written one year before *Kristallnacht*.

While I was in Munich, Wallach's famous store, with its beautiful Bavarian handwoven materials and other handicrafts, was still doing a thriving business. On *Kristallnacht*, that store was destroyed along with the other Jewish establishments.

Within five years of my studies at the University of Munich, on February 23, 1943, a young student there named Sophie Scholl, was beheaded, along with her brother, two other students and a professor. Their indictment read that they "in time of war have promulgated leaflets calling for sabotage of the war effort and for the overthrow of the National Socialist way of life of our people . . . " Sophie was just nineteen when she first got involved with the "White Rose," the name of the movement started in Munich to do something to thwart Hitler and the Nazis. Her writings were edited by her sister, Inge. In the 1950s, I used this book as a text for my German language students. One of the older students said, "Their death was terrible; but, after all, what they did was treason, wasn't it?"

In 1982, the last time I was in Munich, Wallach's store was again flourishing under the same name. The circle in front of the university is now called the "Geschwister Scholl Platz" in memory of that brother and sister who were caught distributing leaflets in the university rotunda.

I want to repeat here what I said at the close of my talk:

> I do not believe that historians will let us forget the holocaust. But, as we mourn and honor its victims, let us do so in a spirit of love and hope. Let us nourish in our children the seeds of reconciliation and teach them by example to work for political, economic and social justice that will not allow the conditions that gave rise to Hitler ever to take root again.

In Munich I attended church more often than at home, and I usually attended the Catholic church. There were many more of them than Protestant churches. I enjoyed High Mass very much. It was beautiful and more moving to me than Protestant services, probably because of the heavenly music. I had a little book that explained the service and was able to follow it with some understanding. It was difficult to be certain how much of my feeling comes from aesthetic appreciation and how much from religious appreciation. I sometimes wonder whether the aesthetic should be separated from the religious to the extent that it often is in our Protestant churches. I always felt in every way uplifted and in much better spirits when I left a service, but I was sure that I could never believe all that a good Catholic believes.

In October Tonino came to Munich for a weekend visit and we agreed tacitly during this time that a future together was improbable if not hopeless. We were both too far along the way to our much-desired careers. Furthermore, that way had been made possible for each of us by others, to a degree too great to allow us to think only of ourselves. Over time, the intense longing I felt changed to a peaceful feeling of gratitude for the beautiful moments we shared during the mere twenty days that we had together.

In a letter to my brothers I described an event three of us observed during a bike trip to the village of Gruenwald in November 1937. We decided to follow soldiers marching toward a large group of people gathered near a new building. There we found many more soldiers, three bands, and a grandstand. The large new building was decorated with red Nazi flags, green spruce, and an evergreen tree. We remembered that there was a tradition that whenever any new building is erected, an evergreen tree is placed at the top of the scaffolding. When the building is finished, the tree is taken down and a big feast is prepared for the workers. Since this was a government building, the new House of Justice, this was an extra-special occasion. Judges in their black robes gave speeches and soldiers marched in, the *Schützstaffel* in black uniforms, the *Schützabteilung* in brown uniforms, the *Arbeitsdienst* in brown knickers and black coats carrying shiny new shovels. Then came the Hitler Jugend (young boys) goose-stepping in. I told my brothers that they would have loved it.

A few days later an even more impressive occasion was the parade and laying of wreathes commemorating the march of the ninth of November 1923 in Munich, where Hitler and members of his party made their unsuccessful attempt to overthrow the government. Sixteen people were killed and Goering was injured when he saved Hitler's life. On Königsplatz the sixteen names were called slowly and the entire mass of party members and soldiers all answered "Here!" I saw Hitler very closely in Briennerstrasse . He made a very good impression, much better than his voice on radio. We had to climb a tall spiked fence (to several onlookers' amusement) to reach a good vantage point from which to watch the ceremony.

During the fall the juniors were treated to an outing, to Bad Tölz to witness the annual "blessing of the horses" by the priest of the local church. The decorated horses and wagons were wonderful—as were the peasants in costumes that indicated the locality, age, and station of the wearers. After the parade, three of us went down into the meadow to mingle with the peasants and "meet" the horses.

November was a month of celebration. Frau Lüttgens gave a party for me on my twentieth birthday, and showed me the material from which she planned to make me a dirndl. Members of the Junior Year celebrated Thanksgiving with a dinner and dance. Since there were not enough Junior Year men, a member of the American consulate introduced several army officers and it turned out to be a gala affair.

Our discussions at the noonday meal were lively. Present at the table were, usually, Kay, Catlin, Herr Blumtritt, Frau Lüttgens, and I. On Fridays, Catlin often started us off. His habit was to spend Thursday evenings at the Hofbrauhaus, where he picked up bits of news that he related to us. We argued over the pictures that Hitler painted when he was younger. Catlin had met someone whose father owned six of them. Would they be worth something someday because Hitler painted them?

Catlin managed to get a press card and rode his bike out to Dachau. But he had no more luck than anyone else trying to get into the grounds of the camp. Every citizen of Munich that he approached hadn't been able to throw any light, either, on what was going on out there. He asked Herr Blumtritt whether he had any idea of the purpose of the camp. The old man shook his head. This was a matter that even he, Nazi pin and all, could say nothing about. What went on remained a mystery also to Frau Lüttgens.

Frau Lüttgens claimed to be "80 percent" Nazi. She said that anyone who lived in Germany between the war and the rise of Hitler and who could remember the terrible inflation and economic chaos would be grateful for the improved economy. She insisted that they could have papered their walls with the amount of money it took to buy groceries. When I asked about the 20 percent of her that was not sympathetic with Nazism, she said, "I really can't go along with the anti-Jewish propaganda prevalent everywhere. I'm like the average Bavarian who doesn't swallow the whole party line—even if Hitler is trying to woo us with stamps calling München the *'Hauptstadt der Bewegung.'* We're not the capital of the movement quite yet!" Her blue eyes twinkled as she continued. "Just you wait until the first air-raid drill. Münchners will never cooperate by retreating to their cellars. Instead, they'll rush out into the streets and look up at the sky to see if anything is going on." (And this proved to be true of the one air-raid drill that I can remember experiencing there.)

* * *

My letters became increasingly filled with pre-holiday excitement, Christmas decorations and festivities mingled with money matters and final exams. Plump Frau Lüttgens was a good friend of both the owner of a butcher shop and the owner of a *Milchladen*. She was thus able to get preferential treatment in this difficult period of food rationing. She was first on the list to receive what was not called for by some pregnant woman or other special person entitled to it. So her boarders could anticipate extra allotments of meats and whipping cream for the coming holiday season.

Thoughts of Christmas mingled with anticipations of a trip to

Italy. We celebrated the evening of the twenty-fourth, exchanging gifts just before dinner. After dinner (two chickens—and very good ones) we drank some Italian light wine with oranges and sugar. Then everyone but me had a smoke while I munched chocolates. It was a very cozy evening. Then we all went to a midnight mass in the Frauenkirche. The next morning we spent lazily at home. In the afternoon the juniors went to the Ruoffs, a German family with ties to the American Du Ponts. Their children, dressed as angels, gave us all lovely gifts. The boys were presented with *Lebkuchen* and knives; the girls with *Lebkuchen* and boxes of soap and toilet water similar to Yardley's. We were served delicious sandwiches and tea. In the evening we listened to the radio and drank beer and cider before catching the train back to Munich. I packed for Italy after I got home that night.

ITALIENISCHE REISE

The train ride from Munich to Florence was long, lasting from 9:00 A.M. till after 9:00 P.M. We were met at the station by Anna Ceresa and our art professor, Dr. Waagen. Anna showed me the city instead of the professor who had mimeographed lists of the places he wanted us all to visit, either with or independent of the group. Every day was filled, from morning till evening, with the search for art treasures interspersed with open-market shopping. Perhaps the most moving event for me while there was the arrival, on the second day, of a card from Tonino, written in Italian. I deciphered eagerly every line, each word evoking tender and affectionate feelings of appreciation for our weeks together. After dinner that evening, I went to Anna's hotel, where we talked at length. Tonino was the main subject, of course, and both of us agreed that his message was a gracefully phrased farewell to a mutually cherished romance. I sent him warm and appreciative greetings by way of Anna. Silently and gratefully, I realized that I had recovered the heart I had "lost in Heidelberg."

Rome was the place where the group said goodbye to 1937, and I celebrated with a letter home:

>   Hotel Britannique, Naples
>   January 5
> Dearest Family,
>   I wish you could see me now. I am sitting in an embroidered silk-covered armchair before the French doors

leading onto our balcony, over which I can see the Mediterranean (as blue as one always hears), with my tired and blistered feet in a steaming footbath! I just returned from a train-trip to Pompeii, where most of the juniors stayed for the afternoon to climb Vesuvius. I can see the volcano from Mrs. Miller's balcony in the next room and it is certainly a thrilling experience to see it covered with snow! Even the Italians are surprised. But despite the cold wind, the sun is shining gloriously warm and splendid in the bluest sky I've ever seen.

I don't believe I had been to the Catacombs when I wrote you last week. Three of us went by fiacre and there the dearest monk I ever expect to meet showed us the underground church of the Christians, their graves, etc. He certainly was cultured and could speak (besides Italian) English, French, Spanish and German fluently. I think it was in the Catacombs that I caught a cold. We were very deep underground and we walked over the cold ground until my feet became almost numb. But it was worth it. It was terribly exciting, too, to be groping our way along with nothing to guide us but the guide's candle and our own tiny ones.

I met Anna again in Rome instead of here in Naples. She came the night before we left and we visited while I packed and showed her my few purchases for her approval. She got up early the next morning to see me off at the station. She is such a darling and I'm happy that I'll probably see her again next July (early) in Munich before I come home.

I must say, we are getting a hundred times our money's worth—the best of hotels, best of service, trips to every museum and place of importance and interest, besides Dr. Waagen's enlightening lectures. I never expect again to have such concentrated pleasure. But I'll have to close. I'll be back in Munich Sunday.

Back in Munich for my second semester, I plunged again into my studies. One course, on the appreciation of music, could be handled in English. The other subjects required nearly total immersion in the German language. Kay was as serious as I was about fulfilling academic requirements, so the two of us spent industriously all the hours needed for our full load of courses, never cut classes, and got our papers in on time. Both of us were excelling in our work. At the same time, an account of the annual celebration of *Fasching* (like a magnified Mardi Gras) showed with what total abandon we were able to participate in fun. Our second semester was marked, too, by the excitement of the annexation of Austria and the Czech crisis, all of which affected student life in Munich.

Back in Munich my letters show that I was becoming increasingly concerned about anti-Semitism. Frau Lüttgens wanted us to talk with her. For the sake of interesting conversation, she did not want us to agree with her, but if we disagreed, she would say that we did not know what we're talking about and should read more. If we quoted what we had read, she would say that one can't rely on what one reads. She knew that I had not been able to accept any sort of excuse for the ugly propaganda in the Nazi press, while she was beginning to swallow quite a bit of it. Her questions required an answer; she asked for my opinion, got it, and then would tell me in so many words that I didn't know what I was talking about. I even agreed to that possibility and said I didn't care to talk about what I didn't know much about. "As a matter of fact," I told her, "for some reason, I haven't met any German Jews that I know of—except for two nice ladies rooming at Pension Hornbeck in Heidelberg."

There was not much point in trying to argue—especially when Herr Blumtritt was present. He thought we were naïve about the "Jewish problem." I did know about anti-Semitism in Baltimore, but we did not make a political issue of it

Kay and I went to see a large exhibition on display in Munich for several months. It was called *Der ewige Jude* (the eternal Jew). The exhibit showed that a great deal of effort had been spent to give a very negative view of the Jews. We attended a lecture on Spinoza at the university, one of a series of lectures on Jews. There was also one on Goethe and the Jewish problem. I did not hear it but read about it in a newspaper article.

Instead of hearing that lecture, Kay and I went to a lecture about education in Germany, and in particular about the *Arbeitsdienst* (labor service). German youth were compelled to spend from six months to two years doing manual labor such as dam building and farming. They lived in large camps, 200 young men in each one. They built their quarters themselves. All wore uniforms and had the strict routine of a soldier without military training and firearms. When they marched through the streets they carried shovels. The training had its good points in that everyone, whether from wealthy or poor families, mingled, worked, and played together. There was something similar to it for girls.

Münchners celebrated *Fasching* throughout January and February, with some event every night for those who had the time, money and endurance to keep it up. During this time, there was absolutely no formality anywhere. The "Sie" form in conversation disappeared altogether and one said "Du" to those who would be perfect strangers if there were such a thing at *Fasching* carnivals. The juniors were so loaded down with work that we did not have time to take part in the celebration. One Saturday, however, the Ruoffs gave a *Fasching* party for us that lasted all night.

We arrived at the Ruoff's home shortly after nine o'clock and found the large house already filled with German people, all in gay costumes. Kay was dressed in a peasant costume of Frau Lüttgens and I wore my Chinese jacket with new black pants that Frau Lüttgens made for me. Bill Sherwood, my pick of the junior boys, was dressed also in a Chinese costume! So, we made a very good pair; and since Bill was a good dancer (he could even do the German waltz—something most American boys could not lead) and also very good company, I was very happy that we were together practically the whole evening.

The party had a circus theme, with paintings done by an art student and one of the Ruoff boys. The Master of Ceremonies was a writer whose last play was a big success. There were a dancing horse (two suffering men) with a beautiful circus rider, acrobats, a circus flea (Mrs. Ruoff), wild animals in a cage on wheels (five dachshunds) and last of all a funny little man on a rooster that laid an egg for every girl who would kiss its bill. The egg was a decorated stocking-darner and made a dear souvenir. Of course, there were circus clowns—two of the Ruoff sons. At four o'clock, Bill and I were still among the up-and-doing. At this time the party was concluded with a group picture. We were at home by 5:30.

Klaus Lüttgens and Catlin took Kay and me to a fest in Schwabylon (Munich's "Artists' District"). We went Dutch (shared expenses); Germans nearly always do. Kay wore the peasant costume again and I wore an empire costume of Frau Lüttgens that just fit me. We left home around 9:15 and walked to the dance hall. Here was real Münchner carnival spirit let loose. I had been warned that it would be a little wild and shocking. The place was filled with laughing, drinking, dancing, jostling, running and, in general, jolly people of all description—in costumes of every possible variety. We started off with a beer. Then one dance after another—around and around in circles till the room with its painted walls and colored lights and laughing people became a rosy blur! Upstairs, where we had our choice of two rooms, each with a small orchestra. Downstairs, in the bar there was still another orchestra. And then back again on the main floor, which had the best orchestra of all. We felt as if we were two Cinderellas who had been taken into an entirely different world. It was fun for a night, but we both agreed that we didn't see how anyone could keep up the pace—every night for two months.

On *Fasching* Sunday there was a big parade with costumes and floats of all kinds, and about fifteen different bands. The theme was quite political. One of the floats had a figure of John Bull as large as our living room. He was seated in all his buxom glory above the crowds with large slices of the atlas in both arms marked "Colonies." At his back was a large box marked "Raw Materials." A pretty good representation of Germany's worst grudge at present. I wrote home that I didn't think they would rest until they had their colonies back.

Another float showed a mammoth suit of clothes made out of wood. Woodcutters were hard at work chopping down more wood for more clothes. Germans were having to make many things out of wood, since they did not have sufficient raw materials, such as wool, and were making synthetics to take their place.

In other letters home at this time, I spoke of my efforts to get reliable news. It was "tiresome," I wrote, "to plough through a German newspaper . . . to read the same political news that is so regulated by the Party that we are sure to get only what 'they' want us to read." There was an American newspaper at the Junior Year, and the London Times. The university library had almost every other foreign newspaper. So we didn't hunger for news. One bit of reading that I looked at askance was put up in glass boxes all over the city so that people were forced to read it. *Der Stürmer* was a newspaper put out by Streicher against the Jews. It was enough to make your blood run cold. Germans themselves were ashamed of it.

My brother David asked about 25,000 strikers being killed. I had not read anything about it in a German newspaper, nor had I heard it broadcast. It was quite possible that there was such a strike. I almost never heard a radio. Frau Lüttgens had none and had to go to a nearby Gasthaus when she needed to hear a speech by Hitler or some other political figure. There seemed to be some sort of block leader who checked to see that "loyal" citizens heard "required" speeches. It was true, I wrote David, about the censorship in Germany—for Germans. I felt free to write what I pleased, however, for our mail was not censored. I was quite sure. Sometimes juniors failed to get certain issues of magazines because they contained anti-Nazi articles. But even that wasn't always true. Kay received a *Time* magazine with an article not at all favorable to the Nazis. Certain articles were removed from magazines in the American Library. Anything that might reach a good number of Germans was censored.

I was no more able to judge Germany's political problems fairly than I was able to judge the political problems of my own USA. All I could do was to keep my eyes and ears open to all sides of every question. That was one reason I was happy to be going to Reisach again for a few days—to hear from Frau Blumtritt an entirely opposite view of affairs from what I usually heard.

On our visit to Reisach, Mary Hoyte and I climbed to the Hummelei—more than two miles—on skis. That would be nothing for a real skier, but it was pretty strenuous for us. We climbed the slope and came down two or three times before preparing to eat lunch. I was pretty disgusted because I had fallen at the bottom every time. The snow was really too soft and my borrowed skis, as well as Mary's, needed wax.

Our lunch time was almost the best part of the day, for we found a perfect Paradise spot. The snow had melted on the hill across the road and the sun was shining its warmest there. We seated ourselves in a thick bed of warm, delicious-smelling pine needles in one of the sunniest patches and had a feast.

It was so lovely that we lay there until four o'clock, when we started home—this time not down the road, as we had done the day before, but through the meadows. We asked other skiers who were going home the same way if it was dangerous for beginners and they said no. Well, it was a little frightening and breathtaking at times, especially when we had to whiz down through an orchard without hitting any trees, or had to zigzag down a very bumpy slope with a precipice and a brook on one side!

We got home without mishap, tired and triumphant, but so late for tea that we didn't even have to get up from the table between tea and supper. We just remained seated, talking with Frau Blumtritt and Eberhard, and went from tea over into supper with no loss of appetite.

* * *

The big news in March 1938 was Germany's invasion of Austria. Reserve troops were sent to the border. The son of the family where Mary Hoyte stayed was among those called up. Catlin, who wanted to go to Italy the next day, was told by the American Consul here that he might not get through Austria. Everyone was waiting to hear about the election there. I really did not think anything very serious would happen—at least as far as we foreigners were concerned.

There was excitement for several days. I was eager to hear what my family was thinking of the news and wrote home that if it stopped where it was I couldn't see but what it was a good thing for both Germany and Austria. Munich seemed to be wild with joy. Those I knew who had gone immediately to Austria were saying that the people in Innsbruck and Salzburg were showing more enthusiasm for Hitler than they did in 1933.

Some juniors were going to Salzburg and I was eager to get their reaction. "At any rate," I wrote, "I'm glad, now that the dangerous part is over, that I was in Germany at a time of such great excitement. Hitler certainly is clever; he couldn't have acted at a better time; the other countries just had to take it."

I wrote of the first Austrian soldiers to come to Munich. They were received with open arms and I got pictures of them. Their knapsacks were covered with flowers thrown by the BDM (*Bund deutscher Mädchen*) as the soldiers went by. I wrote that they "were such young men and looked very shy." I described the excitement when Hitler came back to Munich from Austria: "As soon as the car came into view, the crowds broke loose, running in front of the auto, trying to get to their Führer. The car had almost to stop many times in order to keep from hitting anyone. I never saw people get into such a frenzy. The strange thing is that I got quite excited, too, and could only calm myself down by thinking repeatedly of what all this could be leading to."

* * *

A souvenir of this period was a little picture book. I received it with a loop of string attached so that it could be worn as evidence that I had given to the *Winter-Hilfswerk*—like the poppy we used to receive for donating money on Armistice (now Veteran's) Day. Its title was *Der Führer in den Bergen* and it showed Hitler surrounded by local admirers, feeding a deer, signing autographs for Hitler Jugend, smiling on little girls, staring pensively out over the mountains, appearing everywhere in a charismatic light. I remember how impressed I was by the arrangement by which uniformed men collected weekly on street corners for the poor of the city so that no one needed to beg from the passers-by. Indeed, it was illegal to beg. Only the authorized "collectors" approached the more fortunate, who were given favors of a different sort each week for their generosity. An appendix to this little booklet praises highly the dedication of the Leader to his political duties while vacationing in his beloved mountains, the Harz and Upper Salzburg. I look at this souvenir of fifty years ago with different feelings now.

* * *

I heard the Bavarian minister, Wagner, speak in Königsplatz and saw a big torch parade afterwards. It seemed a little early for a jubilee—but it looked soon as if the rejoicing was quite in order. I read the American paper and was surprised, but pleased, that the USA took it as calmly as it did—I mean, by not considering this the start of another war.

There were loudspeakers all over Munich with jubilant political speeches and patriotic music. It was exciting to march wherever we went. "Wednesday," I wrote, "was a holiday for the schools. Several professors from the University were called to Austria and others are going. All the Germans would like to be there. Klaus is sorry that he just entered military service and was therefore not prepared to go. I wish I could have been in Vienna myself or that I could go at least as far as Salzburg."

* * *

An April letter continued to describe the excitement. "This is another big day in Munich, for der Führer speaks tonight! Just saw some of the political youth heading for an assembly place—bearing big banners: *Ein Volk! Ein Reich! Ein Führer!* I followed them for several blocks, because I still love bands. The speech is at 8:00 P.M. and Dyfri, Marie-Anne and I were planning to go, but we couldn't get seats in the hall—all was sold out. I'm tired from the rehearsal, anyway. So we're not going to mill through the crowds, even if I do deprive myself of hearing more music."

* * *

The rehearsal I was talking about was for a play which the juniors put on for the general public. I played the role of an ingenue in Roderich Benedix's comedy, *Der Störenfried*. The eleven members of the cast represented as many different colleges in the USA. It took a lot of courage and coaching to present this in German, in the Theater im Goethesaal, with costumes and settings from den Bayerischen Staatstheatern.

It was perhaps a good thing that it was a comedy. We all worked very hard to have authentic accents and not confuse genders of nouns. I had one sentence which included "das" Gras, "der" Himmel, and "die"Luft all in a row. During rehearsals, in my struggle to get everything right, I caused the cast to burst into laughter. It became a critical spot for me and I was afraid that the audience would have more to laugh at than the author intended. But I got through the four acts without a hitch on the evening of the performance.

Election Day was on April 10 in Munich. It was a plebiscite asking the citizens for their approval of the annexation of Austria. Marie-Anne had appeared on her bike early that morning. I was always moved by the determination of this curly-headed, tightly wired junior—alert to every possibility of the discovery of new truth. "Come on!" she called, "I'm going to spend the entire day in the nearest voting place. I intend to see for myself just how strictly supervised elections are. I want to know whether we can believe all of the stories circulated about at home and in England." I was not able to go because of play rehearsal.

The propaganda before the election had been very persuasive. Dyfri, back on a visit, had taken a lot of pictures of downtown Munich, which was practically covered with the word "Ja"! "Every store window," I wrote, "all public buildings, streetcars, automobiles, fences—everything was displaying reproductions of a sample ballot with the word "ja" printed twice the size of the word 'nein.' Nevertheless, Marie-Anne reported afterwards that balloting in Munich was as secret as voting methods at home.

June Ebert and several other juniors had returned from a short trip to Austria, where they had tried to see things as fairly and unprejudiced as possible, but it was difficult to understand the complexities of the situation. I expressed my own frustrations in another letter dated April 22:

> "Just got a long letter from Aunt Carrie, raking dictators over the coals and "horrorizing" over the Jew-baiters in Austria. Said she probably knew more about what is going on over there than we do. But when I come home I can assure her that things are certainly exaggerated everywhere—even in the land of the free! Where you read in

your news that toy balloons are forbidden here [rubber shortage], I've never seen more anywhere than on the streets of Munich! Synthetic rubber, of course! And there are other things—more important—that we can see with our own eyes, although I am aware of the fact that there are many things we can't see.

Conversations with Frau Blumtritt and the Quaker ladies in Reisach have made me realize that I'm pretty naïve politically and that I must take some things taught in my German history course with a grain of salt. Somehow, I never ask Aennchen her opinion about things like this. With her Walter in the air corps and her understandable patriotism, I don't feel like broaching the subject since she doesn't, and we always have so many other, more personal, things to talk about—our love for music, especially opera, and our families, etc. I know without asking that she is a generous, tolerant person and could never approve of anti-Semitism.

I'm interested in Aunt Ruth's attitude toward Germany now. Got a nice letter from her a few weeks ago. Remember her dire warnings? Funny how she's changed—but I'm glad. I think she's nearer right now than she was. For Germany's good side has certainly been suppressed in America. I'm not forgetting that there are two sides. It does seem true that once a nation is down, she's stepped on and her first attempts at coming up are discouraged and seriously criticized. But once she gets up again—and if she gets up—then she is respected by those who are compelled to begin to take notice and perhaps be a little afraid. I think Germany is definitely on the uphill grade, and sentiment against her is decreasing at the same rate she is rising. Whether she can continue or not is still to be seen.

. . . I thought of Joe this afternoon as some little boys his age (Hitler Jugend) marched down the street. I'm glad he is in America—even though I do love visiting Germany. I still like the German people as a whole. There's one thing I don't like, however. If I meet two or three men in uniform on the sidewalk, they do not step aside. If I don't want to get bumped into, I have to get out of the way, even if it means stepping off the curb! I shouldn't make generalizations about this, though. I'm sure Walter Kowitz doesn't behave like this when he gets with a group in uniform. . . .

A whole bunch of soldiers on horses and with munition wagons, food wagons, etc. just went by the house. I surely will miss seeing uniforms when I come home. Germany must be the most uniformed nation in the world. Frau Lüttgens says that they love self-imposed discipline over here better than anywhere else. They all love soldiers and drilling, she says.

The rest of the year in Munich went by quickly. My remaining letters included more comments about the political situation but were also filled with more personal reports.

The juniors took a trip to Chiemsee. Every junior could invite a German friend. I invited Aennchen. She had invited me recently to supper with her mother. Aennchen Malmann von Ameluxen was a few months older than I, had a professional education in foreign languages, and was employed as a foreign correspondent for a publication firm. After having met that first time, in the fall at Frau Blumtritt's, the two of us had met again one night at the opera in Munich. Since then, through visits with her in her home, rendezvous at the Café Luitpold, and walks in the English Garden, I was getting to know her well and forming a friendship that was to last a lifetime. Although we rarely discussed current politics, I had the strong feeling that Aennchen shared most of the views of Frau Blumtritt. Her love for her fiancé, so handsome in his officer's uniform, was mixed with a grave apprehension about the future—apprehension expressed more, too, in my letters as one written on May 26 shows.

> . . . A plane is going over right now. I've never seen so many as I have lately over here. And they fly terribly low. Much lower than ever is allowed in America. I'm glad that the Czech crisis is over. (?) One hears little about it around here, but we read about it in the Am. newspapers. And Rollo, an English boy here, got an official letter from England saying that from now on one must have a special visa from England to Germany and that it will be much more difficult for English students to study here. He is lucky to be already here. I'm sure glad I'm an American. It would be terrible to live under such unstable conditions as those existing here now. I love Germany and want to come back someday; but I've learned to appreciate the

good old USA more, too. I didn't realize what little national feeling I had till I came over and saw some of it develop in me.

More airplanes! Kay just yelled from her room, where she's typing, that there must be something going on somewhere. Boy! Am I grateful for my year over here while things are still semi-peaceful. . . .

Along with preparing for and taking final exams, Kay and I filled the last month in Munich with new experiences. We went to the baths, where we spent some time in the women's sunbathing section. On another occasion, when the other boarders were away for the midday meal and Frau Lüttgens did not want to cook, she gave Kay and me money for lunch and we biked to a vegetarian restaurant. We had a "feast" of eggs (scrambled with peas and corn), spinach, carrots, green beans, cucumbers, head lettuce and tomatoes. The quantity was such that one order served both of us for a total of RM 1.20 (30 cents)! And for dessert we had fruit salad: "apples, figs, cherries, orange flavor (we couldn't find the oranges) with whipped cream— about 12 cents apiece!"

I went rowing with Bill Sherwood and a friend in the English Gardens and visited a Nazi Work Camp with the entire group of juniors. I invited Aennchen to supper with Frau L. and was invited again to supper with Aennchen. There was a little Spanish girl there, too She had been here for over a year, a refugee. She had run away with her brother, disguised as a colored tap-dancer in a show going to Africa. They finally got to Germany, where people had been helping them. Their parents were still in Barcelona, and letters to them were returned unopened. And now her brother had just been called to fight leaving her all alone in Germany.

Her story made the war real to me. So did the sirens of the air raid drills that kept me awake from 3:00 to 4:00 A.M. They were practicing for the drill that was to take place in Munich on June 28.

The juniors who could spare the time from their studies were invited to the Ruoffs for one last time. It was a day of sightseeing, in three private cars, visiting "several interesting towns and churches— above all, the Wieskirche, the most beautiful rococo church in Bavaria and perhaps anywhere." Supper at the Ruoffs was followed by dancing and singing accompanied by a guitar. The train got us back to Munich and home shortly before midnight.

I wrote my last letter home from Germany on June 25, describing my final days of exams and preparations for leaving, with Mary, by train for Paris.

There we were planning to stay a week in a pension.

* * *

I waited until I had returned home before telling of an episode at the German border. An elderly gentleman had been seated across from me in our compartment. His grey beard was neatly trimmed and his tall, rather gaunt figure gave the impression of quiet dignity. We were alone except for Mary, who was sleeping. Soon, I began to notice that every time I looked in his direction, I found his eyes fixed on me with an anxious expression. Although, as travelers, we had initially uttered the customary, friendly greetings in German, I was beginning to feel a little uncomfortable under his stare and was keeping my eyes mostly on the passing landscape.

Shortly before the train reached the border, he spoke. "Excuse me, but I have a favor to ask of you." Apparently, I looked somewhat startled, for he continued. "Don't be alarmed. You may be able to be of great help to me." He then went on to tell me that he was a Jew and looked into the corridor apprehensively. He drew three large coins, fifteen marks, from his pocket and asked me to take them through the control for him. They were in excess of what he was allowed and were undeclared. He said that I would not be asked to show my purse. As soon as the officials had seen my American passport, they would be satisfied. But Jews were often searched. I was filled with sympathy and could not refuse. I dropped the coins into my purse and waited nervously.

The transfer was made just in time. A controller stuck his head inside the compartment and with a curt voice asked for our passports. As the old man had predicted, neither Mary nor I was questioned about loose change in our purses. But, to my horror, the controller turned swiftly away from us and abruptly ordered the Jew to accompany him off the train. Without a glance in our direction, the old man left the compartment and was hurried away. In Paris I was always searching the faces of persons resembling him, but I never saw him again.

* * *

The most interesting thing about the voyage home was the exchange of reports and the comparison of events experienced by American students in various areas of Germany. There was considerable contrast between impressions of Nazism in Bavaria and other regions of Germany. I was to remember this contrast many years later when I heard many conflicting tales about "life in India" and could add some of my own, knowing that all were equally true from the varying perspectives.

4

FINDING A FOOTHOLD

1938–1940

No one, I thought, could have said it better than Heraclitus
but was it perhaps the same stream and only I had changed?

For years to come, I crossed the Atlantic by pen alone. Aennchen was, for a while, a good correspondent. Frau Blumtritt answered one letter, but Frau Lüttgens never wrote. The best correspondent, by far, was Dyfri Rees. Our friendship had evolved steadily from the early weeks in Reisach, from our earnest conversations there during private walks together along Philosophen Weg and in Munich's English Garden. While he was back in Oxford, we had begun an extensive correspondence, which we resumed after his visit to Munich in the spring. When it became evident that I was responding warmly to his shy but persuasive overtures of affection, Kay had teasingly cautioned me, "Don't let yourself stumble into 'love on the rebound.' "

Not admitting to the possibility that my warm feelings for Dyfri might develop into a passion approaching what I had felt for Tonino, I paid no attention to the half-serious warning of my roommate. However, when I started to compare his attractions to those of my renounced Italian, I discovered definite similarities. Both had affectionate natures and both were tender toward the sensibilities of others; both were serious and clear about their vocational goals, and even their goals were similar: Tonino was planning to be not only a surgeon, but also a teacher of medicine and surgery; Dyfri would be a teacher of foreign languages. Their physical build was about the

53

same, both being a little under six feet tall and rather slender. Both men were brunette and both had the definite masculine traits of strong chin and prominent Adam's apple.

By the time that Dyfri left Munich after his spring visit of several weeks, I had promised him that I would continue corresponding with him, would consider a closer relationship for the future, and would let him know immediately if my feelings changed. He had given me the same promise. I anticipated a long testing period. It was good that we both liked to write letters.

* * *

Reflecting on my year abroad, I realized that my acquaintance with Frau Blumtritt had helped me more than anything else to understand the political situation. When Marie-Anne had reported that voting in Munich seemed to be as secret as it was at home, Frau Blumtritt remarked that we would have seen a different situation in Reisach where the rural electorate had been lined up to cast their ballots in a fashion that promised no secrecy at all. Frau Blumtritt had been the most critical of all the Germans with whom I discussed politics.

It had been apparent at the university which professors belonged to the Party. They wore the swastika pin and they started their classes with "Heil Hitler." These were the most obvious signs of their allegiance. A few professors had shown no signs of sympathy with the Nazis. One, Professor Borcherdt, had even assigned Lessing's proscribed *Nathan der Weise* to the Junior Year's classical literature course. I wondered later if he assigned this text for his regular university courses.

Wallach's famous store, with its beautiful Bavarian handwoven materials and other handicrafts, although owned by a Jewish family, was still doing a thriving business in Munich. No one was anticipating the infamous *Kristallnacht* of later that year when the store was destroyed, just as other Jewish establishments were.

What began to trouble me most after my return home was my awareness of the anti-Semitism still apparent in Baltimore. Could it ever lead to anything as ugly as the exhibitions I had seen in Munich? And how accurate were the statistics about the relatively high proportion of Jewish influence in the media and the art world of the USA? "Even if they are accurate, so what?" I asked myself. "What does race have to do with talent and ambition?"

I remembered Marie-Anne's wavering opinions and valued

them. Having traveled more than most, she seemed capable of more objectivity than many other juniors. But she had also had an experience shared by no other student in the group. Instead of taking the Italian trip, she had signed up for a ski trip. On the day of departure, she discovered herself to be the only female in a group of about a dozen young soldiers and party members. The ski instructor welcomed her aboard the train and that was the beginning of two weeks of fun and comradeship. She became the cherished sister of them all, endearing herself by performing domestic tasks such as darning socks, and she became a proficient skier as she had hoped. But she found herself also listening to stories of an underground youth movement in which many of these young patriots had participated. They had been inspired to help their country get back on its feet after the inglorious defeat of a great war, the humiliation of an unwanted Weimar Republic, and a devastated economy. As she listened, she felt a growing sympathy for them.

Only after a visit to family friends in Austria, at the close of the Junior Year, did she regain her objectivity. She sent me a postcard with hints of a great change of heart and of explanation to follow later. The father of the Austrian family had been imprisoned and a young relative had been badly beaten for political and racist reasons. The "reunification" of Austria with Nazi Germany, although achieved "bloodlessly," had a dark side. I came to realize that the political situation was even more complex and explosive than I had feared.

It is no wonder that my senior year proved to be extremely difficult for me psychologically. Although the attitudes of Jean and a few other close friends had not changed toward me, many others assumed that I had spent the preceding year absorbing blindly the propaganda of a completely Nazified German people. I was exasperated and upset to a degree that worried my parents as they noticed my growing unhappiness.

Moreover, there was specific evidence that I was not being paranoid in my increasing sensitivity. While I had spent my junior year in Munich, Colette Riley had spent hers at the Sorbonne, and Helen Osborne had spent the summer studying somewhere in Switzerland. All three of us took a course in United States diplomatic history after our return to Goucher. Time after time, the professor would end discussions by asking for the opinions of those who had "been fortunate enough to study abroad," and each time, without fail, she asked in the same order to hear from Germany, France, and Switzerland. Her intonation implied a demand for increasing respect in the progression from Germany to Switzerland. The word from Switzerland always received the crown of her unqualified approval. The professor's bias became the secret joke of the class.

One person understood exactly what I was going through. Dr. Goodloe had taught during the period affected by World War I when there was so much anti-German feeling that German as a foreign language was not welcome in the schools. She had to teach French for several years. She was sensitive to the return of the same feeling toward the German people and their language, but was hoping that educators had learned a lesson about the importance of studying a foreign language, even, or especially, when it is the language of one's current "enemy." Often after class, when we shared a free hour, she would have a sympathetic and supportive talk with me.

* * *

In addition to Dr. Goodloe's friendship and to my immediate family's attempts to bolster my spirits, Uncle Mort and his family were nearby in Bethesda, Maryland, where he was the first head of the Naval Medical Center. Marie was my youngest aunt and seemed almost like an older sister. She entertained with ease and charm, was a devoted wife and mother, and served, along with Mother, as a feminine role model for me. I visited them frequently and enjoyed helping to care for my young cousins. Life there was different, with an international air created by association with Navy families who had lived all around the world.

My connection with this family led to a particularly cheering event among the many discouraging and saddening circumstances at college. Because Marie was at an uncomfortable stage of her third pregnancy, I had another opportunity of the Cinderella sort experienced in Munich. Mort invited Mother and me to use the tickets he had been given for his wife and Grandmother Willcutts (who had been visiting them) for the Army and Navy Ball at the White House. This meant that mother and I could dress up in our finery and dance with our handsome brother and uncle among the uniformed officers and their gaily gowned wives in the East Room. The climax of the evening was the appearance of Franklin Roosevelt, supported by a son on each side, and Eleanor, all of whom waited for a long interval while each guest was presented for a brief greeting. As I stood in the winding line moving toward the president, I felt like a plebeian at court. After FDR's cordial handclasp, as Eleanor Roosevelt's fingers firmly pressed mine and the gracious lady smiled, this Hoosier from Middletown felt the reaffirmation of democracy with its promised opportunities. I knew how energetically this woman continued to work for the fulfillment of that promise throughout the world.

Not wishing to appear boastful about a social event that coincidence had provided and my college friends could not share, I did not speak of this experience any more than was necessary at the time. I had to get excused from a Friday afternoon class with Dr. Goodloe. That was all. My college routine went on as usual, with no more such events, and eventually I did what I had always wanted to do. I changed my major from history to philosophy. This was an easy move because I had already taken all of the philosophy courses needed to supplement the remaining requirements.

From that moment on, I was as happy as I had formerly been with my studies. Dr. Bussey, head of the department, had lived up to all of the glowing recommendations made by my teachers in high school who had graduated from Goucher. She was not only a thrilling lecturer, but she was also a sincere supporter and leader of causes that I wanted to support. She held her classes in such rapt attention that no one was ready for the dismissal bell. The excitement aroused from her Socratic method of teaching lingered until the first opportunity for her students to continue the arguments outside of class, either at a nearby drugstore or the City Girls Center. She was one of the many women who had probably sacrificed their personal happiness as wives and mothers to become completely involved in the movement for women's suffrage. She was an excellent scholar. Her dissertation on freedom had been published, and in the nineteen thirties she was the international president of the Women's International League for Peace and Freedom (WIL). I admired her above all of my other professors and enthusiastically joined the WIL. It was the only such organization I joined while in college. My father did not approve of my joining "political causes" and frowned on "inflammatory literature" that sometimes arrived for me at the home address. "As long as you are living under our roof . . ." was frequently heard that year.

* * *

It was almost taken for granted that I would go on to graduate school. My ultimate goal, I confided to my academic mentor, was to achieve a doctorate and to become a teacher as near as possible like her. "But, Miss Bussey," I went on to say, "I may be aiming for too much. I'd also like to become a wife and mother if I can find the right person."

I was offered two attractive assistantships, one at Indiana University, the other at Duke. My choice was difficult because both schools appealed to me. My main argument in favor of I.U. was sentimental: it would take me back to my native state and I would be attending the university where my father had received his graduate degree. Duke was the final choice: it offered a larger stipend and Dr. Widgery, the head of the Department of Philosophy, had written a very cordial letter suggesting a future at Duke beyond the projected doctorate. If I could have foreseen the future, there would have been another reason for my choice: Carroll Feagins would be there.

Within the week after my parents deposited me in a graduate-student suite that I would be occupying with five other women, Dr. Widgery invited me to his home. Two momentous things happened that night. I met a tall young man with light brown hair, smiling brown eyes, "noble" nose (I like that euphemism for "long and large."), serious mouth, and firm chin. His other arresting feature was his voice, deeply masculine and at the same time gentle. The other philosophy majors, all male as it turned out, were friendly, and the three who were single were attentive. But Carroll made the deepest impression.

The second thing that happened seemed unimportant at the time. Professor Widgery, while making introductions, remarked, "Double names always present a problem. Which are you called, Mary or Ellen?"

"I've always been called Mary Ellen." I answered.

"Well, here you are going to be called Mary. Young men, this is Mary." And then he uttered an obvious cliche, "I'll leave it to you to discover how her garden grows."

This was the first of many attempts at humor that I (from then on and for the rest of my life, Mary) was going to have to endure from this man. He was affable enough, but he was what later on would be called a "male chauvinist." He was proud of his wife in a proprietary way and she was charming and excelled in domestic talents. She was a beautiful hostess and made the students welcome to regular Sunday afternoon teas. Both of them had retained British citizenship along with accents and customs. It was like a weekly trip abroad to visit in their home, and Carroll and I frequently took advantage of their hospitality.

The social scene in which I found myself was unexpected and different from anything I had experienced before. After attending a girl's high school and a woman's college, I was suddenly the only woman major in philosophy in the graduate school. To be sure, the numbers were small, perhaps five or six, but it was a pleasant change for me. I had time for a few Duke football games and once had two escorts for the same game! But I was spending most of my time on class assignments, proctoring, and paper-grading. Within weeks, I had begun my thesis on Nicolai Hartmann's *Ethik*. I had chosen this philosopher rather than my only alternative, John Dewey, because I would be required to continue reading German. Hartmann's *Ethics* was his only work in translation as yet. The fact that he had not emigrated from Nazi Germany had made him suspect. I could find only one article about him in philosophical journals in English, but that one praised his analysis of values and I soon found myself in agreement.

* * *

From our first encounter in the Widgery home, Carroll and I were drawn to each other. I had not felt this way about anyone since my exciting days in Heidelberg and Munich. A reunion with Charles and one or two dates afterwards had revealed the potential for a continued friendship, but any closely shared future was as unlikely as the abandoned one with Tonino. The "romance" with Dyfri could fade, I began to feel, as easily as the ink keeping it alive. I was almost afraid to admit to myself my growing attraction to Carroll. He had knocked on the suite door within a couple of days after our meeting and invited me out "to talk philosophy." We discovered immediately that we had enough to talk about to occupy all the time we could spare from our studies. Often our discussions were closely related to courses that one or both of us were taking or that Carroll had already taken. Most of the time, however, we spent getting to know each other, our backgrounds and aspirations.

For a long while Carroll was an only child. He was nine years old when his brother Walter was born. His mother had said that he had the most beautiful childhood that any child could have. But that, he told me, was her point of view. He had enjoyed playing hymns in his father's church, but being a preacher's kid was not easy. In fact, Walter had announced at an early age that he was "tired of upholding Dad's old propaganda" and Carroll knew what he meant.

Carroll compared the lack of apparent "openness" between him and his parents with what he felt was in my family, but I told him he need not envy my childhood. There had been a lot of exciting arguments, and they could get pretty stormy at times. Being independent, frank, and stubborn as we all were, did not always make for a happy family. David was the only quiet one. Yet, even he managed to arouse our dad's anger when he chose, quietly, to disobey. Mother had a sunny disposition but she also had a temper. She could hold her own in any argument.

Carroll's mother, he said, rarely lost her temper. The strongest words he ever heard her use were "Why, the very idea!" His father just walked out when he saw trouble brewing and worked on his sermons. He could always get his ideas across from the pulpit.

The subject of sex, which we also discussed as we confided our experiences in that area, never came up in Carroll's family. His father's sermons warned against Sodom and Gomorrah with significant hinting about the "fleshpots of Egypt" so that Carroll had come to associate sex with some specific taboos. At the same time, he gathered rather romantic notions from library books.

The more I discovered about Carroll, the more I wanted to be with him. I knew that I had found someone with values and goals like mine. All communications with him fed my growing recognition of an "ideal companion" and aroused unmistakable emotions of love. My feelings in his presence matched those that Tonino had aroused. But until he expressed the same feelings in words toward me, I promised myself to conceal mine.

Carroll made it easy for me to keep the promise. By my birthday, he had spoken those words and we were informally engaged to be married. By Christmas, I was certain that I would be content with a Master's degree. According to my advisor, I was doing good work and I could complete all the requirements for the degree within the year. I was ready to leave formal study and to do whatever would expedite my marrying into my field rather than pursuing it any further myself. I wanted, above all things, to have a share in Carroll's future. I would return to Baltimore, work as a research assistant at Johns Hopkins University for a year, and prepare for the coming marriage. Meanwhile, Carroll would do further work toward his doctorate and look for a teaching position.

5

MARRIAGE, THE EARLY YEARS
1940–1943

On the surface it appeared that we were accommodating our parents' wishes by postponing our marriage a year beyond my completion of the Master's degree. We had each visited in the other's home and each had been assured that the other was a treasure worth waiting for. And when Mother and Ruby, Carroll's mother, got together, they exchanged impressive lists of exaggerated virtues and accomplishments of their two children. I overheard a conversation of this sort and, highly amused, remarked to Carroll, "I didn't know I was getting such a bargain. I trust that you appreciate all my superior qualities, too. Hearing them talk, you'd think neither of us could ever be worthy of the other no matter how long we'd put off the wedding to improve ourselves!"

On closer observation, however, there was sufficient reason for waiting in the fact that economics would not allow us to marry sooner. It took almost a year for Carroll to find a teaching position and for me to earn sufficient funds to give to Goucher the token I could afford in repayment for its generosity toward me. The rest of my earnings I saved for the marriage.

It is an understatement to say that the year was one of unanticipated significance for me. The precision of the word "unanticipated" is questionable. In one sense, this was the time that I had been anticipating all along. But in another, I could never have foreseen the meaningful events and profound agitations of the months ahead.

When the two of us were together, or when I was reading Carroll's letters, I was clear in mind and spirit. I had surely met the someone I had been waiting for. Carroll's appearance in my life had brought into focus all of the loves I had experienced before, to be contained in this one. But when the two of us were apart, I spent hours recalling our experiences together, evoking the emotions they had produced, and wondering.

Fortunately, my job in the graduate school of Johns Hopkins University kept me very busy. Professor Carl B. Swisher was writing a book, *The Development of the American Constitution.* As his research assistant I was allowed to do a little of the rough drafting of one or two of the chapters in addition to doing research and typing. I loved the work and learned a lot. I decided that I might like a permanent job as researcher if I did not find what I wanted in teaching. I also made good friends among political science and economics students working near me in the stacks of the library.

One such friend, bearing the name of my younger brother Joe, held great attraction for me and contributed to the "wondering" I was feeling. Rather than describing our relationship, I prefer to share a poem written during the months preceding my marriage. I gave it to my friend.

THERE IS A LOVE APART

There is a love apart from that dear love
Compelling man and woman to embrace,
To live their lives in unison, to trace
A single pattern as through life they move.

A love so boundless it will soar above
The waves of passion, share its time and place
In infinite encounters, face to face,
While seeking quiet like the peaceful dove.

It finds and knows its object, still withheld;
And here it stops. For it must not possess.
The only joy allowed is to behold.

If, in beholding, such love is beheld,
The love is even greater. Nonetheless
Demanding more will cause it to grow cold.

The year passed by rather quickly even for me, never known for my patience. Carroll's rare visits to Baltimore were always occasions for celebration and frustration. As I faced the prospect of leaving Baltimore for a life with Carroll elsewhere, I was eager to introduce him to my favorite haunts. We spent one delightful evening in The Peabody Book Shoppe, which was not at all what that name implies. It had been a speakeasy during the days of Prohibition but was now a place to eat and to listen to live music, usually string. Another favorite restaurant was not so conveniently located. A long streetcar ride to the waterfront was required to reach Haussner's, a wonderful German eating establishment that offered much more than its superior cuisine; it was also famous for its large collection of varied works of art.

I treasured another occasion, afforded by Uncle Mort. Three former juniors from Munich days were converging on Washington, D.C. for a reunion. My uncle arranged for us to have lunch at the Army and Navy Club, thus adding a little glamour to the day. It was a happy reunion, the only one that I would have with Kay, June, and Marie-Anne together.

The day of the reunion ended on a less glamorous note. I had an attack of what resembled appendicitis during the preceding night, which I had spent at my uncle's home in Bethesda. By morning the pain had subsided and I had forgotten the episode. However, my surgeon-uncle had not. As he was preparing to drive me to the station for my train-ride home, he suggested that we stop at the hospital for some tests. This detour led to a phone-call for my parents' permission for him to operate that very evening! The fact that he performed the operation with a local anaesthetic, allowing me to witness the entire procedure, did add some glamour to the event, after all. The fact that Aunt Marie was in the same hospital with a new baby was cheering. Best of all, Carroll took time off for a special visit.

I stopped work two weeks before the date of the wedding, September 10. Professor Swisher's book was almost ready for the printer. (He had used it as a text for his course and injected some humor into it by reading my typographical errors, for which my friends in the class expressed their gratitude.) My assistance was no longer needed and a friend and I spent a week at the beach for a much-needed rest. Not long before I left, Mother brought a stack of invitations ready for Dad to post.

The days preceding the wedding were hectic. Carroll's parents came a few days early and were staying with us. His father was performing the ceremony, with the local pastor pronouncing only the necessary words to make it legal in Maryland. He had written out the entire service and had given it to us for our editing and approval. We did make a few changes, primarily to suit our aesthetic taste, but also to please my parents by using my complete given name. The exercise was in vain, however; for when the day arrived, the Reverend Feagins had his original wording already so firmly embedded in his memory that he did not vary from it in the slightest.

The ceremony, everyone said, was beautiful in its simplicity and sincerity. It was something for me to remember with deep satisfaction. Jean was my only attendant and Carroll's best friend, Tom, recovering from a bout with jaundice, returned from Mexico just in time to be his best man. David, having been inducted into the army a few days earlier, had to risk being AWOL for the occasion. Joe and Walter, Jr. served as ushers. They threatened some practical joking but kindly refrained, after all. Because another usher had been called away at the last minute, I prevailed on the friendship of Joe Loftis, a political science student at Johns Hopkins, to serve as substitute.

Two memories of that day amuse me now, although one of the incidents did not strike me as humorous then. At one point during the service I was to put my arm through Carroll's. When we reached that point, and I started to make the proper gesture, Carroll thought my move was premature and held his arm so tightly to his side that I had to pry my way in! 'Even if he's right and I'm wrong," I remember thinking indignantly, "he ought not to make an issue of it." I felt real anger at a moment when my heart should have been full of love. My feelings soon changed to more appropriate ones, however, just as they were to vacillate easily many, many times in the years to come.

The other incident amused both of us, and perhaps Dad, too, although I forgot ever to ask him. The "father of the bride" was determined that there would be no undignified tomfoolery to spoil the sacred aspect of our marriage. So, he suggested a hiding place for the car that Carroll had borrowed for our honeymoon. It was in an alley nearby, and Dad was to help us make a quick getaway after the reception in the garden behind our house. All went well until we transferred to our little roadster. Just as we drove away, Dad's arm must have hit his car horn, which became stuck. Thus the newlyweds left with an inordinate amount of noise provided by the very one who wanted quiet.

There was one other incident relating to our wedding day that we learned about later in a letter from one of our closest friends of Duke days. Ed Flud Burrows had been in the graduate school studying history. He had become well-acquainted first with Carroll, later with me, and had been my welcome partner when the infrequent opportunities to dance arose. Carroll did not share my enthusiasm for dancing. He, like Dyfri, preferred to express his rhythms at the piano or organ. He seemed to enjoy watching his two friends waltzing about the floor more than he enjoyed taking the lead himself.

We three friends had arrived independently at a firm position against the impending war. We were convinced that violence, especially killing, provided no solution for the injustices we wanted to see eliminated. Each of us had arrived at the position by a different route, although our arguments all had roots in the New Testament, specifically the Sermon on the Mount. Not one of us was willing to condone or participate in the killing of others who were thrown by birth accidentally into the ranks of the "enemy." Ed, being single and with no intention of marrying, had already been drafted as a conscientious objector (C.O.) and was serving in a Civilian Public Service Camp near Marion, Virginia. He wrote Carroll on the night of September 10 that he had stolen some moments at the time of our ceremony to find a secluded spot, on a rock at the edge of a stream, with a clear view of the mountains. There he read through the Episcopal marriage service and was with us in spirit. We remembered this when, several years after the war, our paths converged at Guilford College to remain close again throughout our years of teaching and retirement.

We spent our honeymoon in a cottage on the Holston River, where we could swim and canoe, walk over a romantic hanging bridge, and enjoy a week of bliss. Not very many years later, the Holston was dammed by the Tennessee Valley Authority (TVA) and this idyllic spot disappeared under water forever, like Brigadoon or Germelshausen, to rise to the surface only periodically in my memory.

Directly from there, we went to live in Bristol, a charming little city cut in half down its main street by the Virginia/Tennessee border. It was beautiful among the mountain "knobs" in the spring, summer, and autumn, but not so beautiful under a cloud of soft-coal dust in the winter. Carroll had been invited to join the faculty of Sullins College, a private academy and junior college for young ladies that had recently earned a superior academic rating through the efforts of a new young dean. We found humor in the fact that Carroll's new position was going to fulfill an extravagant promise he had made during courting days: he would see to it that I would not be burdened by too much housework. Part of his salary came in the form of board and room for the two of us. Although we were given a modest apartment soon after the initial few months in a crowded "teacherage," there was not enough work required to keep me busy with domestic duties. Any cooking I did was in connection with entertaining a few relatives who lived in Bristol—primarily to prove that I really could perform in this area. But cooking was a luxury we could not afford very often. We were provided with good Southern cuisine in a dining hall, with service worthy of an antebellum plantation. Carroll's small salary made it equally impractical to dine out. (Soon he began to supplement his income by playing the organ and directing the choir in a Presbyterian church in nearby Abingdon, Virginia. He was to use his musical talents in this way throughout most of his teaching career. The additional income allowed us a little luxurious living now and then.)

For two years, I had all the time I could want for reading. I finally completed *War and Peace* among other books I had put off for just such a time in my life. Furthermore, both of us were invited to play in the newly formed Bristol Symphony Orchestra. My violin parts had to be simplified by the energetic young conductor, who thus showed her friendship and, probably, her desperate need of performers! Carroll brought more talent to the group with his quick adaptation to the viola. It was a happy time for me, especially after I became pregnant during our second year of marriage.

Only one thing marred our happiness—Carroll's reclassification and impending induction for active alternative service. There was a bright side even to this, however: the president of Sullins College had promised that when Carroll was drafted, I could take over his classes because my qualifications were in the same field of study as his. Others, too, seemed to support Carroll's pacifist position. One friend, Helen Barns, was, like us, a member of the Fellowship of Reconciliation and the War Resisters' League. She had declared privately her own pacifist position. She taught biology and could avoid injecting political or ethical subject matter into her classes. Carroll's teaching of religious and philosophical subjects made it impossible for him to avoid ethical questions, so his views were quickly known although he was careful not to advocate them in his teaching. He used the Socratic method, drawing out all sides in search of possible answers to a question without providing dogmatic answers. Because of his reputation as an excellent teacher, he was called on as a public speaker, and so his views became even wider known. The respect that he earned helped dispel our dread of the separation that his alternative service was soon to bring about.

Meanwhile, on June 10, 1943, one year and nine months after our wedding day, I presented Carroll with a son. (Mother had actually counseled us to allow the marriage a year for adjustment before starting a family, but it was coincidence and an early spontaneous abortion, not exact calculation that brought about the precise date of this event.)

I had seen x-rays of the baby. At first, as I recalled pictures that I had studied in the old family encyclopedia and in more recent ones, I had not been able to distinguish our son (I thought only in terms of a boy after a prediction based on the rate of heartbeat), but when Dr. Gammon said the baby was in an upright position because he was breeched, I saw immediately a perfect profile of the head. Now I felt already acquainted with the little creature.

During labor I felt only twinges of pain, not enough to groan about. In fact, I was beginning to look forward with increasing impatience to each contraction. Finally, in early afternoon, Dr. Gammon appeared and said, cheerfully, "Let's get you upstairs where we can have a little privacy!"

The delivery was too interesting to allow for much experience of pain. In a pleasant cloud of chloroform, administered in modest doses by an efficient hand, I was able to assist consciously at the birth of the reluctant offspring. I had to laugh when the doctor announced the confirmation of my baby's maleness, the first sign to show itself. After his full appearance, head last, he was whisked away immediately, and I fell asleep.

I learned from the nurse that Carroll, Jr. had experienced a good deal of trauma during his early hours, almost not surviving them. Holding him in my arms for the first time, I felt his strangeness, his fragility, his need for my nurture. Suddenly, as I was looking at his faintly yellowed face, he began to gasp and to choke. I felt his entire body jerking in spasms. Before I could utter a sound, the nurse, still standing by my bed, snatched him quickly from my grasp, turned him upside down and began pounding his tiny back. I could not suppress a cry of alarm.

"Look," the nurse almost barked at me, "if you're going to behave that way, I'm going to take him out of here right now." Seeing me get control of myself, she continued to spank the tiny infant. "It's nothing but fluids; he's going to be O.K. See." She handed him back to me. "You can have him a little longer, but you won't be nursing him till next time I bring him."

I looked at my son, now quiet and breathing evenly. How easily I could have lost him! I would have to take special care of this baby. If he was to belong to Carroll and me, he would not be like any other possession we had ever shared. "Responsibility" would be a better word than "possession"; for, if he made it through infancy, he would belong ultimately to his unique purpose in the world. As parents, we should try to help him find it.

As for myself, the androgynous self that I had felt for so long became forever manifest. Not only did I express this in poetry; I was also moved to express this same spirit a few years later in a carving of Honduran mahogany.

ANDROGYNY

Beides war ich,	I was both in one
erst durch ein Kind	until a child
und die Gerburt ist mir	until its birth
das Andere offenbart.	disclosed my otherness.
Im Schatten bleiben doch	And still unclear remain
die Grenzen	the boundaries.

6

ALTERNATIVE SERVICE

1944–1945

As the day of Carroll's departure for Civilian Public Service approached, I began to notice a change of attitude in many of our friends. They did not express outright disapproval of the position for which they had known all along he had registered, but a few began to indicate some surprise that he actually was going through with it. They were a bit cool toward him, seemed to be avoiding his company and mine, too, until after he had gone. This was in January, 1944, and by this time Carroll, Jr. was six months old. Friends began rallying around me, expressing sympathy for the new mother and baby who had been left on our own.

Helen Barns was the only colleague at Sullins College whose attitude toward both Carroll and me remained the same. She had become almost like family. Her generosity toward us as newlyweds had included the down-payment on a Steinway upright piano, which had the interesting feature of having once been a player-piano. All she asked in return for this was permission to "come and lean on it once in a while." Sharing our views toward the war, she could understand our feelings precisely. She had sat up late with us on the evening before Carroll's final physical examination at the time of induction. We had discussed the ethics of his using his susceptibility to asthma attacks as a possible means of avoiding service altogether. If he exercised strenuously just before the exam, he might easily bring on an attack. But, since his records already indicated a history of asthma (without any detailed medical records to back it up because they had been lost) and the draft board had chosen to ignore this, the three of us decided against this strategy. Carroll laughingly related afterwards that he really had suffered an asthma attack on the way to the center because of the brisk walk in the cold air; however, waiting around in the steamy, warm room before the exam, he had nicely recovered to pass it with no difficulty.

Helen was my chief means of moral support in Carroll's absence. She baby-sat during the hours when the employed nursemaid could not be there. And she listened to my lesson plans for a course in economics which Carroll was scheduled to teach and for which neither of us was especially prepared. Without her love and kindness, this time of separation from Carroll would have been much more difficult to bear. As it turned out, the busy teaching schedule along with my care of Carroll, Jr. made the days pass quickly. Carroll's frequent letters describing his new life in CPS, working under the supervision of the National Park Service at Gatlinburg, Tennessee, helped to keep me happy.

Then, one day in March, the letters from the college administration offering contracts for the next academic year arrived. I opened mine with the assurance of seeing in print the verbal agreement Carroll and I had already reached with the president. But this is what I read:

> Sullins College
> Virginia Park Bristol, Virginia
> March 22, 1944

> Mr. & Mrs. Carroll S. Feagins
> Sullins College
> Bristol, Virginia

> My dear Mr. & Mrs. Feagins:
> These are critical days for our land and Sullins College. Her teachers, her students and her patrons believe that we are fighting to save everything which is prized by civilization.
> Knowing your honest convictions about this war, and knowing your sincerity in teaching, we have definitely decided that we cannot offer you an engagement for another year.
> This decision has been reached after long and serious

deliberation and with fullest consideration of your high ideals and of your excellency as instructors.

You are regarded by our Faculty, by your Colleagues and by the Students as among the best teachers on our staff and your steadfast character commands the respect and esteem of all of us at Sullins. While this is true, the Faculty and Students are practically unanimous in feeling that the winning of this war should command our utmost effort, and that there should be absolute harmony at this point.

We want you to regard all of us as your friends who are ready to render any possible assistance, and when our righteous cause has been won we will be glad to work with all our might against war, which we all regard as the greatest curse of the world today.

Sincerely yours,
(signed) President

I could hardly believe that the highly-respected president, who had even claimed anti-war views and pledged sympathetic support for Carroll's stand as the only appropriate one for a Christian (he, himself, was a Methodist Sunday School teacher)—this man who had allowed me to step into Carroll's classroom so that not one day of class was missed, was now going back on his word. Quickly, I went to find Helen, who had received a similar letter of dismissal. Our initial shock and dismay gradually changed to anger.

Carroll managed to get leave in order to come home to see what he could do to remedy the situation. The two of us made an appointment to see the president, and he asked us to come to his house. "I am as sorry about this as I can be. I wish that it could be otherwise," he began.

"But you promised!" We were speaking loudly and almost in unison.

"I did not foresee what would happen. I have received countless letter from parents saying they did not want to keep their daughters in a school where pacifism during wartime is openly countenanced and supported."

"You know, this is a good case to be censored by the American Association of University Professors," Carroll said angrily.

At this, the president replied with equal intensity of feeling. "I'm not afraid of any investigation by the AAUP. We've dealt with them before and we've survived." He calmed down and began to speak with more sympathy. "You don't need to worry, Mary. I know that your parents will be glad to have you and little Carroll come to live with them for a while. It's Miss Barns that I feel responsible for. Her pacifist leanings wouldn't even have been known if she hadn't come out so openly in favor of your position and hadn't been seen so much in your company, attending Fellowship of Reconciliation and War Resisters League meetings and the like. I am truly sorry that I have to let her go, too. But I have to, out of fairness."

We were not comforted by his words. We were still feeling wronged and indignant. I was thinking that I ought to resign tomorrow, that I had just been a convenience to the school. They did not have to find a replacement for Carroll for the rest of the year. If I resigned I would make it hard for him right now. However, I said nothing and left with Carroll when it became clear that our protests were leading nowhere.

Upon investigation, it became clear that we wold have very little chance of academic or other redress for this kind of discriminatory practice during wartime. Helen agreed. We would finish the school year as professional ethics required. Soon, the president substantiated his declaration of responsibility toward Helen. He found her a good teaching position at another private college. He continued to display sympathy toward me, but he insisted that he was sure Carroll, Jr. and I would be better off at home with my parents than with my having to combine teaching with motherhood. He did not seem to understand what a blow to my pride it was going to be to have to seek parental help from either the Browns or the Feaginses, especially since they did not approve of Carroll's position.

My father had said to Carroll in his usual blunt fashion: "I concede, it's a Christian thing to do. But it's most impractical—a damn foolish thing to do. You'll never be able to get a decent job after the war. Why don't you apply for 1A-O classification and go along as a non-combatant? You could probably play in the band or something."

My mother felt pretty much the same way. Carroll would at least receive an army private's pay if he registered as a noncombatant; whereas, at the camp then under jurisdiction of the Quakers, he was getting something like $2.50 a month for incidental spending money. And now my salary would no longer be available. But Carroll could not conscientiously accompany troops who would be actively engaged in killing.

In my family, only Grandmother Willcutts and David gave unqualified support. Grandmother had come to visit soon after Carroll, Jr.'s birth. At the time, she had expressed pride in what she considered "real courage" on Carroll's part for taking such an unpopular stand in wartime, when it really mattered. She did not think much of "peace-time pacifists." It was ironic that David, in the army, was getting such an unexpected version of the trip to Germany that I had wished for him. He reminded us that he had been drafted and would never have volunteered. He sent a check for fifty dollars from overseas "for diapers for little Carroll" and had written supportive letters. Joe stayed quiet on the subject. He had joined the air corps, but was disappointed that poor eyesight had prevented his qualifying to become a pilot. He wrote that he was "planning to become a gunner and fly over David's division, or one like it, as protection." He did visit Carroll's camp, however, on a trip to Knoxville.

I could not understand why Carroll's parents were not more supportive. Apparently, they were like many other advocates of the Christian religion who put the Sermon on the Mount aside for the duration of the war. They seemed actually ashamed of our position, I discovered later when I accepted their invitation to visit them in the pastorium at Clearwater, Florida. Whenever local guests were present, my in-laws immediately began to talk about their other son, Walter, who had joined the navy and was assigned to the postal services. Some church members were thus led to assume that little Carroll and I belonged to Walter. I had to enlighten them to the fact that my husband was the older son, Carroll. For several weeks, I went along with the Feaginses' silence as to his whereabouts.

Finally, one day when I could stand the subterfuge no longer, I said to Mother Feagins, "I am not at all embarrassed by Carroll's conscientious objection. I agree with him and am proud of him. I am not going to sit quietly by and let you and Father Feagins hide his light under a bushel—especially after reading Mrs. Bladen's letter to the editor in yesterday's newspaper. She may be a star member of the congregation, but I can't ignore her diatribe against the COs in a Florida CPS camp where a good friend of ours is serving." She asked me to talk to Carroll's father. He wouldn't discuss the subject with her. Furthermore, he refused to read the newsletter from Gatlinburg. She did, at least, read it and tried to understand.

I tried to talk to my father-in-law, but it only upset both of us. I begged him to preach just one sermon on Jesus's sermon in Matthew, to see how he could interpret it any differently from Carroll. No matter how much I tried to persuade him, he never chose that text during my visit. Finally, one day, he declared, "If you don't stop thinking and talking about this, it will drive you crazy!" That revealed a lot about his own state of mind.

What did have some positive results was my gradual revelation to members of his congregation about Carroll's alternative service and that I shared his views. The Reverend Feagins was surprised to hear one of his favorite Baptist followers, an outstanding member of his church, say fervently: "If I were a man, that's exactly where I'd be!" From then on, although he never shared Carroll's point of view, he was not as reluctant as he had been to talk about it, so long as there was no argument. I avoided the subject with him, however, because I was always inclined to argue.

* * *

Carroll and I said to each other more than once that we were glad that each of us had reached our stand against war independently and before we met. Neither of our sets of parents could accuse either one of us of having led the other astray. We were in agreement about objections to the war. This does not mean that I, as a CPS wife and mother, did not have to face questions on the subject outside of the family.

"What are you going to tell your son someday when he asks what his father was doing during the war?" The question came from Wilhelmina, a young woman whom I met almost daily on the beach. I took Carroll, Jr. there by city bus on weekday mornings to relax in the sun and enjoy the lunch of boiled custard and sandwiches that Mother Feagins helped to prepare. Wilhelmina had a son who was the same age as mine, and the two toddlers were enjoying their parallel play while we mothers talked.

I knew that the question was meant seriously and kindly. My new friend's husband was in the army and was a source of pride for his wife. She was trying to understand a position that seemed most unpatriotic to her, if not cowardly. But she knew that there must be some sort of courage involved in a stand that met with such general disapproval. I had already explained the nature of Civilian Public Service. It was a chance not provided during the First World War. If it had not been for patriots like Norman Thomas, who had gone to prison as the only alternative to supporting the wholesale killing of enemy patriots, the opportunities available now in this war probably would not have existed. I told her that their patriotism demanded a critical evaluation of what their government was engaged in. If they could not support it, they were obliged to try to change it by means of democratic action or by civil disobedience, if necessary. My words, as I remember them, seemed to be arousing some understanding in my listener as I continued:

We're fortunate to live in a democracy, I know. And I know that your husband is fighting to preserve our democracy. But democracy is meaningless if it is not practiced—both in peace and in war time. We are acting according to our conscientious beliefs, as is your husband, I assume. We are implementing a law enacted by democratic means to express our disapproval of war and support of democracy. I don't honestly believe that I'll have any trouble explaining this to Carroll, Jr. when he is old enough to ask the question.

Wilhelmina did not bring up the subject again. We remained congenial companions for the seven months I spent in Florida. How I would explain everything to Carroll, Jr. was not the question that began to gnaw at me in secret. Sometimes I asked myself whether, if I were a man, I would not have joined the armed services as a noncombatant. I dismissed the question as irrelevant when I began to notice that this question seemed important usually when I was bemoaning the fact that there was not governmental support for conscientious objectors outside the military while there was a private's pay for those inside.

I was bothered by another question, one that could not be answered until after the war was over. Did the stand against the war really count for anything except on an individual, almost insignificant basis? I remembered a young man in political science in the graduate school of Johns Hopkins. He had discussed the CO position with me earnestly, and had said, "I am joining the Navy. I would take the CO stand if I thought it would count for anything. If I knew for sure that there would be even as many as ten thousand objectors to this war, I would join their ranks. But the time is not here yet. There are too few of us. It's not worth the grief it would cause my parents. They'd never understand."

I regretted very much the grief Carroll and I were causing our parents. In some respects, the Sullins College president had been right. My parents had welcomed me and their grandson, whom they would get to know much better this way. At first, Mother had even offered to give up her first job outside the home in order to take care of little Carroll while I worked. In fact, I went so far as to get a job with Baltimore Friends School one day, but gave it up the next. Mother reconsidered and decided that she should not give up the first job Dad had ever allowed her to take. She loved her work as director of a children's war nursery, which provided for working mothers who were filling the jobs of men in the armed forces. It would be better for me to stay home and look after my baby.

I certainly could not argue with that. Then Mother came forward with another proposal. She was too tired at the end of the day to feel like preparing much in the way of dinner. She would pay me a little if I would tidy up the house and fix the evening meal. I was very grateful for the suggestion. There was valid reasoning behind it. It also helped to preserve my pride if my parents did sometimes remember our discussions of Carroll's CO position. Not once did either one say, "We told you so."

I remained with my parents from June until Christmas. I felt I could not turn down any longer Carroll's parents' repeated and urgent invitation to come to them for the holidays and a month or so beyond.

I might never have gone if I could have known that it would take many months before I could move with Carroll, Jr. to Knoxville, where I planned to find work as soon as he was old enough to place in a nursery school. Carroll would begin the search for a job and housing as soon as he could adjust to his duties at the camp in Gatlinburg and get leave to take the bus to nearby Knoxville. He found me what seemed an ideal position as an assistant in a nursery similar to the one Mother directed in Baltimore. Finding housing was more difficult. The woman who arranged for the job also pursued the search for housing and solved that problem quickly by locating a development for those in "war services." The nursery was under these auspices. I made reservations for the train to Knoxville and looked forward to the end of a visit that was becoming too long for both Carroll's parents and myself. Then came the blow. When the concerned authorities discovered that my husband was one of "those COs out at that camp," they declared that I did not qualify for either government housing or the nursery for children of war workers. The helpful social worker who had so willingly made all the arrangements was embarrassed and indignant at the decision. She liked Carroll and sympathized very much with his concern for wife and son. She wrote me an apologetic letter and Carroll began the search again.

When a camper received a medical discharge and his wife left her apartment in Knoxville, I was finally able to move there, place our son in a nursery, and begin my own search for a job. Carroll and I still had $200 in savings, mostly from the sale of furniture in Bristol. I had to find work before this ran out. I avoided jobs of a public nature, of course, after my experience with public housing and the nursery. I was being considered for a radio job or a teaching position at the University of Tennessee, for neither of which I had experience or special qualifications, when I was told at the employment office to apply for what I was best qualified to do, public school teaching. The need there was great, they insisted, and there was where I obviously could be of most service. I tried to explain my reluctance to pursue this possibility but was advised to try. I did and I got the job that I needed for financial independence from our families.

There was one string attached: I was not to tell what my husband was doing. The public school employment officer had just employed another CPS wife and knew that he was allowing the shortage of teachers to influence his decision to make these unpopular appointments. I abhorred the subterfuge but agreed to respond to any questions with the misleading answer, "I am not free to talk about this." Unfortunately, too often, the assumption was that Carroll was doing some secretive war work, perhaps research at nearby Oak Ridge. It was not until after the Christmas holidays that a colleague of my age, of whom I had become fond, was able to guess (at my request) that Carroll must be at the Gatlinburg camp about which an article had recently appeared in the *Knoxville News Sentinel*. From that time on, I felt quite comfortable in my work, even though I did detect a little coolness from one or two teachers, whose opinions I did not value anyway. My best friends were understanding, if not approving.

All things considered, the year in Knoxville, at Christenberry Junior High School, was a rewarding one. I discovered that I loved teaching and felt that I was cut out for that role. I became particularly involved with Jerry, a student of English, who had been labeled "delinquent" by his former teachers. I learned that he was easily motivated if encouraged in his creative writing. I struck a bargain with him. If he would do his assignments in grammar, I would read and criticize his short stories. The caliber of his work never led me to believe that he would have any success as a writer, but I felt a sort of pedagogical triumph as I observed the happiness he was deriving from my encouragement and noticed some progress in his grammatical constructions.

Carroll, Jr.'s year in Knoxville did not appear to be as happy as his mother's. Weekend visits to Gatlinburg were pleasant for both of us at first, but soon the change in altitude and temperature began to bring on regular attacks of asthma, sometimes causing him to have uncomfortable Mondays at nursery school. Even the fact that a thoughtful camper devised and built a little sedan chair with which Carroll and he could carry our son for hikes up and down hill did not prevent asthma. Eventually, we had to give up these trips and to look forward instead to less frequent visits by Daddy.

Knoxville was not nearly as pleasant for our reunions as the beautiful campsite. I missed the relaxing weekends. I found, to my sorrow and deep concern, that I could become more impatient and desperate than was good for either mother or child. Our son refused to go to bed at night without crying and seemed to be satisfied only with a spanking on his tender behind. This was a carefully administered spanking, which became almost a ritual without any visible physical scars, but which brought anguish to me even when I rationalized the temporary "habit" as necessary for the sleep both of us needed.

Perhaps his happiest times were spent walking to nursery school with Shirley, the CPS wife who shared our apartment and taught nearby, and playing under the supervision of loving nursery-school personnel. One young couple was especially devoted to the children, and Carroll, Jr. looked forward to their attention. I like to believe, when I look back, that he can also remember the hours I did find for him to read stories, to sing, and to try to teach him, by means of his two little trucks, to learn the colors red and blue. This last, I believe, I began too soon: he was still confusing those two primary colors after he had become familiar with all of the others.

The end of the war came without too great sacrifice on the part of either of his parents. There had been one critical time toward the end, when Shirley's husband was released from CPS and I was left suddenly with all of the rent to pay. However, Carroll's father had begun to send a small monthly stipend by then and the Quakers had provided the extra amount needed, just as they had helped others in financial trouble. I can look back now with gratitude for many things. We had made friends and enjoyed experiences that would influence our future in beneficial ways.

We had a relatively easy transition to postwar living. Carroll had temporary work for the American Friends Service Committee in Philadelphia while we "house-sat" in Haverford for a Quaker family and waited for a new position at Guilford College in Greensboro, North Carolina. Carroll had become acquainted with this Quaker school while at Gatlinburg and had even taught a philosophy course for the camp in its extension program, dubbed "Rufus Jones College' by the participants. Our unhappy departure from Sullins College had receded far to the back of our store of memories. The future held promising challenges that we looked forward to meeting. Dire predictions of scarce job opportunities for Carroll had not materialized, thanks to the Quaker administration of Guilford College.

Much to my peace of mind, also, I was given evidence that Carroll's CO position was correct. It so happened that the best way for such a position to count—and to be counted—was probably the way he had chosen. The numbers of men who participated in Civilian Public Service were carefully kept by the National Service Board for Religious Objectors. Those who took the position of noncombatant in military service had no control over the keeping and the releasing of figures. If counting was important, those who took the CO position numbered more than the 10,000 required by my friend who had joined the Navy. It was clear that there must have been many, many more objectors than were ever revealed by the Selective Service System. This should encourage those in the future who have to face conscription and who might otherwise fear that conscientious objection would be a futile gesture by an insignificant few. I no longer doubted that I would take that position myself, if I were a man.

7

SORTING MY SELVES

1941–1956

From the day of our marriage and for many years to follow, I was happy to be known as "Carroll Feagins's wife." I felt a surge of pride when I first used the words "my husband." It took sometime before I could use this term without conscious pleasure in my new role. After Carroll, Jr.'s birth I felt deeply enriched by the added dimension of parenthood. The periods of enforced separation for weeks, sometimes months, only enhanced my appreciation of being a part of Carroll's life, sharing with him the responsibilities of a new family. As a human being, I felt complete as never before.

It seemed natural and likewise fulfilling to become a "Faculty Wife" at Guilford College. Our group of women was closely knit and had a significant part to play in the community. We greeted newcomers to the campus, co-hosted students who met in our homes for seminars and social occasions, provided refreshment for bloodmobile volunteers, and shared hobbies with those of similar talents. I was both amused and annoyed at the strict limitation of membership, under the leadership of President Milner's wife, to wives of professors only. Wives on the faculty without husbands on the faculty were excluded! This presented some embarrassment because one professor, the sister of a faculty wife, could not belong because her husband, although well educated and a good friend of the college, worked for the local telephone company. Such discrimination was eventually done away with after I and other faculty wives invited several women faculty members when it was our turn to entertain. They became regular attenders and eventually the group became the Faculty Women.

I was also known as the wife of the organist at Wesley Memorial Methodist Church, in nearby High Point, where Carroll served for several years. His avocation of music offered me the opportunity to be audience and appreciator as well as to share the company of many friends acquired in this connection. It was a fringe benefit that I valued highly in our marriage. I would never forget, either, the time Carroll spent during our early years together in encouraging me to participate in music-making. He bought easy arrangements of two-piano and organ-piano pieces and spent hours playing with me. In spite of his encouragement, I gradually gave up the idea of playing with or for anyone. I preferred listening to the more talented, and finally, played the piano only rarely and when alone.

Saying that I was content, indeed very happy, to be known as Carroll Feagins's wife is not to say that I did not feel loved and appreciated for myself. But my self was a much more domesticated self than I had ever pictured myself becoming. I was continually surprised at the amount of pleasure I derived from cooking and entertaining. I enjoyed even doing the laundry and smelling the incomparable aroma of clothes fresh from the lines where they had absorbed clean air and sunshine. Ironing was something I learned to like when I perfected my technique of folding and ironing clothes efficiently.

Carroll and I planned from the outset to have three or four children. Just as soon after CPS as we could live together again, and with the security of Carroll's new position, we decided to have our second. Early in 1947 we knew it was on its way. Meanwhile, a new discovery had been made, news of which came out in *Time* magazine soon after I had verified my pregnancy: the RH factor. I learned that I was RH negative, while Carroll was RH positive. The possible consequences gave some cause for alarm, but my doctor was prepared for a transfusion if necessary and I approached the time of delivery with little more fear than I had felt before Carroll, Jr.'s birth.

We did not own a car, but Carroll was promised the use of "Beulah," a Model-A Ford belonging to a student, who with his wife, the college nurse, shared a campus house with us. In addition, I had bought Dr. Benjamin Spock's *The Commonsense Book on Baby and Child Care*. I loved my obstetrician. Dr. Burwell called all his mothers-to-be "Honey" and, I was sure, made them all feel equally safe and cared for. He also showed respect for a woman's intelligence and carefully explained every aspect of what was to be expected. He and I had only one slight disagreement. I insisted on natural childbirth with no anaesthetic. He preferred to plan on a delivery as painless as possible. He did not like to rely on my assurance that I, personally, had not experienced much pain at my first baby's birth and was glad to have been conscious for his arrival. After much persuasion, he agreed with reluctance to allow me this opportunity for a second time.

After it was all over, I felt that everything had gone very well. St. Leo's Hospital had been a wonderful place to have a baby. The Catholic sisters were competent and serene. I welcomed the religious atmosphere, as I remembered how I had been deprived in Bristol of the quiet which would have enhanced my first experience in a labor room.

David Willcutts Feagins was named for his great-great-grandfather. That David Willcutts had inherited a corner cupboard that, in 1815, had journeyed westward with his father, Thomas Willcutts, and other Quakers who were leaving the institution of slavery behind in North Carolina. The corner cupboard had returned to the East with Sue Willcutts Brown, my mother, and was supposed to be inherited only by a Willcutts namesake. I wanted it and used this way to assure it for my own family. I was also happy to have a namesake for my first brother and was looking forward to possible namesakes for Carroll's brother Walter and my own Joe. Now, however, I was content to concentrate on the two sons who were already here and were quite enough to occupy my loving attention.

I was never sure when I first began to notice dissatisfaction growing within myself. In a spell of self-probing, one day, I discovered that I was not entirely happy with being known primarily as Carroll Feagins's wife and the mother of his children. I was missing something. When I found myself, for example, with Carroll as a part of a foursome including a husband and wife who were both on the faculty, I often felt left out of something shared by the three of them. It was a vague feeling, sometimes remaining at a subconscious level, but surfacing again when Carroll was in the midst of musical or pedagogical discussions with colleagues and seemed not aware of my presence. I enjoyed listening to subjects that I was keenly interested in and ventured contributions whenever I felt like entering the conversations. Nevertheless, I began to feel more and more like an outsider—except for the times, in our own home, when I was playing the role of hostess, or when I was spending time with other faculty wives and their children.

Perhaps this had started before David's birth. A strong feeling of nostalgia had been aroused in me when I had received a letter from Jerry, the mislabeled "delinquent" of Christenberry Junior High School. It had been painstakingly written in his best penciled long-hand on lined paper.

>   Knox., Tenn.
>   341 W. Atlantic
>   Feb. 10, 1946

Dear Mrs. Feagins,

I suppose you're wondering what that old pest, Jerry Madden, is doing writing you. The fact is that I regret not having treated you with gratitude inccount with your fine help and support with my ambition to write profitable and famous novels. At the first of school I was looking forward to further help from you but when I discovered that you had moved I was very disappointed. As I look back now I appreciate your help very much and in dedication to you I am going to dedicate my first book to you. By the way, what is your first name? If I ever become anything in the field of authorization I will always remember your fine consideration and will speak of you in a thankful tone.

I was going to come to you in person and ask for your help, but when I asked Mrs. McPheeters where you lived and she acknowledged me to the fact that you were out of state I desided to write you. By the way, have you noticed that my vocabulary has increased? This also came about as a result of your cautions. But I still don't like it although I have arrived to the point that I know a good vocabulary is very useful in this profession.

A few of my latest and best novels which I have completed are:

While The Sea Remains
Guardian Angel
Black Dust
Adventure Beneath The Sun
Safari Assignment
Raccial Conflict
Glory In A Sanctuary

Little Pedrow And The Curse Word
Texas For Conquest
Destroy The Flame

The teacher is watching me so I will close for now. And write soon.

Gratefully,
Jerry

I had laughed as I shared this with Carroll. "It's good to see that I've inspired at least one student! I do miss teaching. When Carroll, Jr. is older, if we don't have more children, I want to return to the classroom. Even if we do have more family, I want to teach again when they're old enough, of course."

Jerry was to reintroduce himself to me in the 1970s as David Madden, established writer of stories, plays, novels and literary essays. His writing had appeared in scholarly and popular publications such as the *Journal of Aesthetics* and the *Best American Short Stories 1969*, among others. In one of his novels, *Bijou*, I appear as Miss Redding, his eighth-grade English teacher. He contacted me while he was writer-in-residence at the University of North Carolina at Chapel Hill and was invited twice to Guilford College to read from this and an earlier novel, *Cassandra Singing*. On the flyleaf of my copy of the latter he wrote words of appreciation and tribute which I have stopped to reread with pleasure and will cherish always. It strengthened my ambition to teach again.

* * *

I had answered Jerry's letter at once and stored it among my souvenirs of CPS days. David had arrived before the year's end. Carroll seemed to have become content with our life just as it was, keeping happily busy with his teaching, occasional public lecturing, and music. The supplementary income from the organ playing, though small, was useful for extra family expenses and occasional outings, like visits to Baltimore and Clearwater. But I began to notice the increasing amount of time that he was spending playing duets and two-piano numbers with Phyllis, the wife of the couple mentioned above or practicing with musically talented students for college performances. I saw that it was gradually replacing his plan to complete the doctorate interrupted by our marriage. Time was running out.

I had to admit to myself, and even to Carroll, that I was envious of Phyllis, who complemented Carroll so well musically. Although I assumed that Phyllis was as devoted to her husband as I was to Carroll, I was beginning to resent Carroll's blindness to the fact that the three of them had more in common than I was able to share and that I could not enjoy their times together as much as he did. Yet, he was encouraging more frequent bridge games and suppers with the couple in addition to the hours spent with Phyllis alone.

Carroll did not seem as much concerned as I was about the deadline which had to be met for the completion of the work begun at Duke and to be finished now at Northwestern. So I kept bringing up this subject and urging him to explore the provisions made by the college for a leave and for financial support to complete the degree. President Milner had jokingly said: "Guilford can't afford to buy PhDs, so I'll just have to grow them!" Very generous arrangements could be made if Carroll would only take advantage of them in time. After several unpleasant scenes that ended often in angry tears from me and silence from Carroll, we reestablished the neglected goal as a priority and took the steps needed to reach it.

When I remember my admitted jealousy of Carroll and envy of Phyllis's relationship with him, I can never be sure how much weight these feelings carried in my persistent drive toward what seemed to be a worthy, if not essential, goal in connection with his academic promotion. Part of my motivation was doubtless my eagerness to find a teaching position for myself, which would supplement our income. Because of this need for more income, I had now a legitimate excuse, in any case, for pursuing something I wanted in addition to domestic life.

I found out about a position even sooner than I expected. Walter Coble, a member of the local school board and New Garden Friends Meeting, on hearing of my desire for a teaching position, told me of an opening for a fifth grade teacher at Guilford Consolidated School in the coming fall. He advised me to apply immediately, which I did. Because of my master's degree, I qualified for an Emergency-A certificate, a rating created during the war to help alleviate the shortage of teachers. With this I would receive the top salary for one of my experience and could be used at any grade level without penalty to the school employing me. I considered myself fortunate.

Once again, I had reason to be thankful for association with the Quakers. I had joined New Garden Friends Meeting the year after our arrival at Guilford College. A coincidence had made this easy to accomplish. I was substituting one Sunday for the teacher of a Quaker adult class and, after the lesson, a discussion led to the subject of evangelizing. "Friends do not believe in proselytizing," one member of the class insisted. Evelyn Haworth, a respected member of the meeting and a faculty wife, had gently remonstrated. "That is often said. However I believe we Quakers sometimes overestimate the value of this restraint. In our eagerness to refrain from urging individuals to join and to wait for the initiative to come from seekers, we may seem to be unwelcoming. Reluctance to apply pressure on anyone should not prevent a friendly invitation to join."

These words had made me feel free to ask, "Just how does one join Quakers?" Carroll and I admired what Friends stand for and agreed with what we knew of Quaker beliefs and practices.

Carroll had waited for a while to join, out of consideration for his father's position as Baptist preacher, but it had not taken me long to write the necessary letter of request to the clerk of the meeting. A committee of three members soon called on me to welcome me into New Garden Meeting. The Quakers did not claim to have rigid answers to my questioning mind. They welcomed me as a member who could share what enlightenment they might have as we continued to seek further together for the leadings of the Spirit. So I felt at home in the Religious Society of Friends. My search since childhood for a religious group to which I could honestly and wholeheartedly belong was ended.

Although Carroll would not leave till the following school year, I soon discovered that it was to his advantage as well as mine for me to resume my teaching career while we would be together. There was a good deal of family adjustment to be made during that time. Carroll, Jr. was attending the same school and could ride the two miles to and from with me. David's care presented a problem. This was solved when Janet Hilty, a faculty wife, offered to look after him during the hours he could not be cared for in New Garden's cooperative nursery school. I soon became accustomed to coming home with the children and exchanging news of the day while I prepared the evening meal.

In order to supplement our income further, we had taken in a boarder, Dr. Muriel Tomlinson. She was Professor of French, somewhere in her thirties and prematurely gray. Her sense of humor was infectious, so her company was welcomed by those around her. She liked to hear and could tell a good story, with one stipulation. As she put it, "I don't mind a little dirt once in a while. But I do insist that the dirt be refined."

Anticipating the need of even further income and recognizing the advantages of having a man about the house, we accepted the offer of Ed Burrows, our friend from Duke days, to become a second paying guest at the Pines, our college house. He had recently been added to the faculty in the Department of History and had already distinguished himself among colleagues and students alike. When Carroll and he approached President Milner to sound him out concerning Ed's staying with me while my husband was away, the President assured them, "As long as it's Ed, I can approve." The Pines had been built for a large family and had enough bedrooms and bathrooms to have served previously as a small dormitory. In fact, both Ed and Muriel were such congenial additions to the Feagins family that they remained on for some time even after Carroll returned.

This second extended period of separation from Carroll was more difficult for me than that of CPS years in several respects. He was too far away at Northwestern University in Illinois to afford more than one visit home, for Christmas. For the first time, I was assuming all the responsibility for our household accounts. Moreover, although Ed and Muriel were undemanding boarders for breakfast and supper, I missed Carroll's presence at this time even more than usual during their discussions at table of college matters that did not concern me so closely now. Ed was especially helpful as baby-sitter, but he could not quite take the place of a parent when it came to counsel and discipline. I had to become father in addition to mother as the boys looked to me for all provision and guidance. (After Carroll's return from Evanston, it was to take months of constantly referring them to him, to break their habit of turning to me for everything.)

Regular letters from Carroll described a busy course of study, with some fun in between, reminiscent of Duke days. I longed to be sharing in person his new experiences, missed his tender voice and touch, and sought comfort in the company of our friends—especially Ed.

If I ever became completely myself, it seemed to be while I was forgetting myself, and this happened best in the classroom. Here, I was totally absorbed in the present situation—in the exchange of ideas, in the excitement of discussion, in the use of my talents and in the demands for my total attention to the young persons temporarily under my care. These demands for attention sometimes led to discipline problems. It occurred to me, at some point in my thinking, that I might meet these challenging problems with greater success if I kept the implied meaning of "discipline"in mind. Wasn't this the necessary factor for creating disciples? Not my personal disciples, but disciples of truth. If I could guide my charges to become aware of their unique potential and if I could transfer their attention to the need to respect others and to the virtues of cooperation and compromise, they might become too involved in their common goals to vie for my personal attention in undesirable ways. I dedicated myself to becoming a better teacher by starting each day with the intent of making my students disciples instead of "making them mind."

No matter how many days I started this way, however, there were almost as many that ended on a very discouraging note. Somewhere along the line of lesson plans, one or more of my little disciples got out of step and managed to trip up my equanimity. Reminding myself that I believed in the possibility of constant rebirth rather than the finality of being "born again" once and for all, I continued to start each day with hope.

One friendship, especially, brightened my years of teaching at Guilford Consolidated. This was an experienced and naturally gifted teacher of the sixth grade. Mary Ella had a beautiful sense of humor enhancing her genuine love of children. She had also a beautiful farm and rustic husband to go home to every evening. Along with pigs and poultry, they had two fine horses, a Tennessee Walker and "Lady," who was just that—a gentle mare most suitable for someone like me. Often, Mary Ella and I would ride together early in the morning before school. On these days, I would get up at three-thirty, put on the only pair of jodhpurs I ever owned (dating from my rides with Charles in York, Pennsylvania!) and slip out of the house without waking the family. My friend taught me to catch and saddle Lady and led the way on her own "Tennessee" down the lane to the country road, one of the few as yet unpaved. After such rides, I would return completely relaxed and ready for whatever the day might present.

This was the one close relationship I had independent of Carroll. Even so, he became acquainted with her, as I became acquainted with Colonel, Mary Ella's husband. He was a man out of a different century. He should have been born at the time of Andrew Jackson, or earlier. His virtues were those of a pioneer. He had driven most of the nails into their magnificent farmhouse himself, although Mary Ella had shared in the planning and building. He loved to hunt, declaring that the barking of hounds during the night (a nuisance to me) was the sweetest music to his ears. He was famous for his cooking, especially for his Brunswick stew. I learned to like the accent of peppercorns and other spices that I had not used in my kitchen. Although I continued to be skimpy in the use of spices while the boys were growing up, I did not forget in future years what I had learned from Colonel's kitchen.

I had one other cause to be grateful to this colorful countryman. It was a crude but pertinent comment that I was to recall many times in my public schoolteaching career. The boys and I were spending a rare Saturday at the farm. Mary Ella had taken each of the children for a ride in the sulky, holding them between her knees. Upon their return the boys had remained outside to entertain themselves by the pond and to explore other sights and sounds of the farmyard. Colonel and I were chatting in the living room when my friend walked in. I greeted her with the admiring comment that she amazed me with ability to spend every weekday with her sixth graders and then on weekends to invite children to her home—to fish or ride or do whatever delighted them.

She reminded me of how much she and Colonel had wanted children of their own—how disappointed they both had been when she discovered she couldn't have any. He enjoyed them as much as she did.

I turned to Colonel and continued to speak glowingly of her way with children. She had such fun in the classroom and seemed always to have her kids in the palm of her hand or hanging on her words and laughing at her jokes. They never got out of hand. And she really taught them—to read, write poetry, dance and do arithmetic. And they loved it.

She smiled at my words but admitted that she had to "bark at them" sometimes, had to threaten to "knock a knot" on one or two of them. Her reputation for fun without foolishness had grown over the years. I expressed my despair of ever achieving her skills as I asked, "Doesn't she ever come home and cry on your shoulder, Colonel, the way I do on Carroll's?"

"Nope," he replied, "never! You know what your trouble is? You seem to forget you're not married to the little bastards." Both shocked and convulsed by his remark, I laughed at the comforting thought. I never forgot it. Time and again, in the midst of a frustrating encounter with an unwilling "disciple," I would say to myself: "Remember, Mary, you're not married to him!" And then I would laugh to myself, freed from close personal involvement. When such children no longer felt they could hurt or upset me, they found the challenge less interesting and returned to more fitting group behavior.

Carroll returned from his year at Northwestern in 1952, with his preliminary exams behind him and his dissertation to complete at home. I stopped teaching as we had planned I should when we could do without my additional income. I was torn psychologically between my two careers: while teaching I had feelings of guilt that I might be neglecting my role as wife and mother; while "homemaking" I had feelings of unfulfillment. Both were sublimated in the desire to have at least one more baby. By this time, I was dreaming of a daughter or two. I even wished for twins, like my Grandmother Willcutts'.

There was an unhappy surprise in store for me. Soon after my pregnancy was verified by Dr. Burwell, I experienced an early miscarriage (technically, I was informed, a spontaneous abortion) like the one before Carroll, Jr.'s birth. Although I took all recommended precautions after the first signs of trouble, I lost the baby. Weeks of sadness over this event were followed by weeks of hope for another, this time successful, pregnancy. But this was never to come about. Unlike most women, at the age of thirty-six I found myself unexpectedly on the other side of the menopause. Hormone treatment was not indicated, according to the doctor, and a period of treatment with a thyroid compound proved futile. It began also to affect my heart adversely, so it was discontinued.

Sharing my sadness, Carroll agreed to my idea of adoption. We both were thinking of a daughter, now that we might be able to choose. Unfortunately, adoption at that time was not easy. So many more couples were desiring babies than there were babies available that agencies had made a rule giving preference to those without any children. After months of frustration following our formal application for an infant daughter, we were finally discouraged from any idea of increasing our family. I went back to Guilford Consolidated to replace an eighth grade teacher on maternity leave. It was a long time before my feeling of deprivation turned into a feeling of freedom.

A fortunate set of circumstances helped to bring this about. In 1955, our good friend and boarder, Muriel, decided to leave Guilford for a position as head of a newly formed French department at a university in another state. At the same time, there was going to be a second vacancy, creating the need for a teacher of German. Since both Muriel and the departing German teacher knew firsthand of my training and fluency in the two languages and were willing to recommend me to the Department of Foreign Languages, I was offered a non-tenured but full-time position as Instructor of French and German. I began teaching my first course at Guilford College, an intermediate class of eight students of German, during the summer of 1956. From then on, problems of classroom discipline were, for me, all in the past. Nevertheless, I would always be grateful for my experiences at the fifth grade and junior high school levels, feeling I had become in that way better able as a college teacher to understand the educational background of my students. I had already learned, too, that my public school teaching made me more objective in my relationship with our two sons. In comparison with most other children under my care, I found our sons' social behavior quite exemplary and began to accept with an enlightened sense of humor some of the things that had formerly caused me to worry.

Of one thing I had become sure: there is no greater challenge than that offered to public school teachers, when they are expected to devote an entire school day to their pupils—during classes, during recess and often during lunch hours. I remembered them with appreciation as I enjoyed continuing their work at a more advanced academic level. And I even had the occasional pleasure of teaching French or German (even both, in a few cases!) to students I had taught in the fifth or eighth grade (even both, in two cases!).

Another source of great satisfaction at this time was the gradual development of another lasting friendship with a young woman, Polly Cobb, who resembled Marie-Anne Greenough of Junior-Year days. The resemblance was not so much in looks (although there was a slight resemblance) as in manner, interests and enthusiasm.

Polly had learned as a child to speak not only French, like Marie-Anne, but German as well and had been exposed to an international culture. She gave the impression of robust health because of the energy she exhibited in the various activities she pursued. I learned, however, that she had gone to Tucson, Arizona for a year of graduate study in music theory and psychology primarily for her health. She suffered periodically with asthma, like Carroll and Carroll, Jr., and she had had a particularly trying summer in 1939. In Arizona she had met Whitfield Cobb, a brilliant student/instructor of philosophy and mathematics, with whom she developed a serious relationship, fostered by long letters when he returned to Chapel Hill. After a year, she enrolled at the University of North Carolina for further graduate work and the relationship was continued. Whit, like Carroll, had been a conscientious objector serving in a CPS unit attached to the Duke Medical Hospital. He and Polly had married immediately after the end of the war. Whit was invited to serve on the Guilford faculty not long after we had arrived. It quickly became clear that he and Carroll had much in common besides Civilian Public Service and the four of us became fast friends.

Polly shared my interest in German and French and, in addition, became fluent in Russian. She had Marie-Anne's enthusiasm for political and social action and she drew me into some civic activities that I might otherwise have missed. One of these was scouting. I actually became an active "den mother" serving for two years with Polly in the care of scouts aged six to ten, including George Cobb and David among the older ones.

Some of my happiest days were spent with Polly and those cubs. I increased my knowledge of birds, rocks, snakes and stars. Best of all, this involvement served as a bridge between teaching and homemaking. At last, I had reached the point where I could pursue a double career without feelings of guilt.

8

LOSSES AND GAINS

1956–1963

When I joined Carroll on the faculty of Guilford College in 1956, we experienced two great losses. His mother died in the Bristol hospital where Carroll, Jr. was born. She, along with Carroll's father, had been visiting her sisters and their families when she was seized by a heart attack. That, complicated by a worsening diabetic condition, brought about her unexpected death.

Ruby Feagins had always been very private about her long struggle with diabetes. She was quite in contrast to my diabetic father, who let all around him know with strong expletives when his daily self-injection of insulin went wrong. No one could honestly say that it was a "blessing" for her to be taken, at the age of 61, from a "life of suffering." She had been a model pastor's wife, had sung in the choir, and had used her sense of beauty to decorate the church and pastorium for weddings and other celebrations. I could not remember her without a flower in her hair, often a gardenia from the garden she loved to tend. A snapshot taken of the three sisters only a few days before her death shows her cheerful disposition when they were together. I would miss her.

In 1957, my father died. I was thankful that he had lived long enough to take pride in his son-in-law's Ph.D., which he had not been able to achieve for himself, and in my own appointment to the college. He had also seen the beginnings of a new house, which Carroll and I were having built on the edge of the campus. We had planned for it for several years and would be able to pay for it before our retirement. My father's death was sudden, also from a heart attack, but it was not unexpected. Although he had continued to head the Department of Vocational Education at the University of Maryland, the daily effort was becoming more difficult with the increasing ravages of diabetes. One of his favorite friends, a longtime secretary, said to my mother that she could tell how he felt and what sort of disposition she could expect from him each day by the tilt of the fedora that he always wore.

He had been granted a one-year leave in 1941 to serve as Maryland State Administrator of the National Youth Administration. This program had given many college students, including his daughter, an opportunity to earn part of the fees needed to pay for their education. It was scheduled for termination by the end of that year. Because of the coincidence that this was the year of our marriage, our wedding had received more notice in the Baltimore paper than it otherwise would have and the mayor had signed and mailed us the newspaper photo. I was grateful that my father's colleagues had honored him shortly before his death with a testimonial banquet. Too many times such recognition is put off until it has to become a memorial celebration.

As I was receiving the stream of visitors at the funeral home and listening to their tributes to my father as teacher and counselor, I felt pangs of regret that I had never accepted his repeated invitations to visit his class as I waited for a ride home with him. Instead I had chosen to read in his office. I had never heard him lecture, and had only read and heard accounts of his ability to stir audiences with his philosophy of education. A single red rose in a bud-vase on the mantelpiece, with a card "from a student," touched me more than any other floral arrangement in the room.

Immediately after Ruby's death, Carroll's father came to live with us. He had a room and adjacent bath at the Pines and then moved with us to the new house beyond the college lake. There he occupied the "grandparents' apartment," originally planned for extended visits by both sets of parents. In accordance with his well-established custom, he announced his intention to do all the dishes. This was of great assistance to me, whose domestic help since I had begun teaching consisted of the faithful Monday-morning energies of Viola. She was the regular right hand, also, of two other faculty wives, the president's wife, and Ed Burrows. (Ed, also, had a new house near the campus, which was too much for even a domesticated bachelor to manage alone.)

* * *

Viola McAdoo needs a biographer all her own. If anyone is to be credited with making her own way, and blazing the way for many others, against the obstacle of being black in a white society, it is this strong-willed woman. Her church was, materially, less than a mighty fortress, but it was, spiritually, her steady bulwark. She drew the white families for whom she worked into the support of its ambitious activities by her dauntless solicitations. She was as appreciative as she was aggressive. Her sense of justice was acute and she did not hesitate to "fuss and bam" until a wrong was made right. Then she would express her thanks with all her heart.

Her husband Wil worked in a small grocery-store across the street from the campus. By combining their meager earnings, the two of them succeeded in building a modest cottage on their own land, doing most of the work themselves. I remember our being guests for supper with them soon after its completion and admiring their comfortable furnishings. Viola confessed to me that the first time she sat in her new tub in the midst of all that indoor plumbing she had "bawled like a baby" with happiness. She and Wil encouraged two adopted sons (the children of a younger sister who had died in childbirth) to finish high school and then saw them through North Carolina State University of Agriculture & Technology. Wil was a quiet, dignified man, who exhibited his thoughtfulness when I attended their elder son's high school graduation by following me home in his car, in spite of my protestations, because he did not want me to drive through their neighborhood alone that late at night.

At the graduation exercises I was impressed by the enthusiastic support of parents. There were more fathers present than I might have anticipated, had I not already observed a strong sense of family and a high percentage of good marriages among the black community in our area. In contrast, a number of white children of the area who were bussed to Guilford Consolidated came from families of poor background and squalid living conditions.

How could I ever understand, then, the reaction of our community to the Supreme Court decision requiring integration of the public schools? I knew that the school bus would be picking up children from mostly respectable black families now in our district as well as the wide variety of white families included. Carroll and two other members of the Guilford College faculty, Whitfield Cobb and Hiram Hilty, who had children in Guilford Consolidated, sought to encourage a quiet acceptance of local black children to their school. They wrote a letter to the school board assuring their support of the North Carolina Pearsall Plan, which left the implementation of the Court's decision up to local school administrators. Polly, Janet, and I signed the letter along with our husbands. It was shown to a few sympathetic neighbors who signed it and suggested others to be given the same opportunity. Altogether, there were only thirty-three signatures when it was delivered. Within a couple of days, a "leak" to the local newspaper appeared in headlines and the community was immediately in an uproar. There was a frantic gathering of over three hundred signatures (I recognized children of school age among them) for a "petition" protesting the acceptance of black children without a specific court order and indicating a fight against that as well. As a matter of fact, on the first day of school a crowd gathered before Guilford Consolidated. They were white families. A few angry fathers even carried hunting rifles, and a local preacher encouraged the group to stand firm against any black parents who might try to enroll a child. No black parent appeared that day.

No one would have expected then the extent of ugly behavior in what had appeared to be a peaceable community. The signers of the letter (all listed in the paper) were harassed, especially those native to the area, who were looked upon as traitors to Dixie doctrines. Dynamite exploded in the driveway of one family with five children. A furniture dealer received anonymous threats against his little daughter and was boycotted by a group of former customers. The one good result, he remarked, was that many who owed him money paid up old debts before quitting his store. One young man lost his job and most of the other signers, including the Friends pastor and wife, received angry phone calls. Even the membership of New Garden Friends Meeting was, for a time, divided on the issue. One Quaker told Carroll, "You and the other signers have set race relations back fifty years. I'm afraid a few heads will roll at the college."

I recall a conversation with another member that I later reported to Polly. "You integrationists surely must realize," he had scolded, "that the colored children would be out of their element and really be unhappy being forced in with white children. For one thing, they'd not have proper clothes to wear."

That remark was made at a New Garden Friends committee

meeting and I was delighted with my own rejoinder. "That just isn't necessarily so, Friend. I know one little girl who'd feel right at home. Her mother works for Polly Cobb and Polly's daughter Jane, wears her daughter's outgrown dresses. They're that pretty and durable." I laughed as I reported to Polly how speechless my illustration had made this Friend.

Only the efforts of a few peacemakers, who opposed the letter but believed in freedom of conscience, hastened the healing of the breach. President Milner's policy of supporting the conscientious political and social actions engaged in by members of his faculty, no matter how unpopular, was vigorously tested at this time and was reaffirmed, much to the relief of the concerned signers.

Viola never reprimanded Carroll and me, as she had felt free to do on occasion, even though the publicity aroused a redneck element of her neighborhood to cowardly acts of vandalism meant to inspire fear in the blacks. I had excitedly reported to her how we had been awakened during the night by that terrible explosion. "We sat straight up in bed, it was so loud. And it came all the way from the Meredith's house! Someone had thrown sticks of dynamite and blown a large hole in their driveway. Just because they'd signed our letter! As if all the threatening phone calls weren't enough!"

There was only a gentle chiding in Viola's reply. "Now you white folks know what it feels like to have no-account trash speeding by in their cars and yelling threats, waving guns, and shooting at mailboxes in the night. This isn't the first time for us, you know."

But she smiled sympathetically, for she understood and appreciated our good intentions. It was our best attempt to act openly, and now legally, to remedy the hopeless racial discrimination surrounding us. Our past attempts at social action—boycotting all but the one movie theater that allowed integrated seating, helping to organize an inter-faculty forum among the three white and two black local colleges, having "mixed" conferences in our home with overnight black guests,—had been small gestures in comparison to the sit-ins at Woolworths that would take place not far in the future. And we had not had to pay significantly for our involvement.

I recall that this was the occasion for my first letter to the editor—as a former teacher in the local school. I wrote that I knew firsthand that an editorial, lamenting the predictable "lowering of educational standards" by the admission of black children, was completely wrong; in my own eighth-grade classroom I had taught "white" children with reading levels ranging from third-grade to eleventh-grade. I was sure there would be children from the black families who would fit in at all levels.

When the time came, a year later as I remember, for local blacks to feel ready to enroll their children, integration was achieved without any noticeable difficulty. The aroused community had had its opportunity to release tension. Moreover, of the three hundred or so signers of the petition against integration there had been one or two families represented who felt out of place among the poorly educated and prejudiced families making up the majority of names. They were visibly embarrassed by the newspaper publicity.

Only one faculty couple at Guilford had suffered unexpected consequences for their participation in social action for better race relations. Chauncey Ives had been brought to the college in the early 1960s to head the English department. He had immediately joined forces with those who had supported desegregation by organizing the Inter-Faculty Forum. His concern for racial justice was open and intense. Although not an active member of the Society of Friends, he stemmed from Quaker ancestry and soon made it clear that he could not tolerate the fact Guilford, a Quaker college, was not integrated when he arrived. That schools in the South might have more difficulty in taking this step than schools in other areas did not deter him from making his views widely known. The fact that he had come recently from outside made his views more unacceptable than the same views of a few other faculty members who were already using their persuasive powers to influence the trustees of the college. When time came for a tenure decision, Chauncey Ives was denied it on grounds that he was an unsympathetic teacher. Both Carroll and I were among those who knew this could not be substantiated. The exact opposite was true. We were joined by a number of tenured faculty members as we called upon President Milner to protest the decision. A group of students, both weak and strong academically, also crowded into the President's office to support their teacher and protest his dismissal. If the decision had been left to Clyde Milner alone, Chan and his wife, Jane, would have remained. But others were adamant in their disapproval of the awarding of tenure.

After it became evident that the Iveses would have to leave the home, which they had just built in anticipation of a future at Guilford, Carroll and I became totally caught up in their misfortune. We realized that our friends had advocated the same views as our own and were, in a way, scapegoats for several tenured faculty members who might justly be faring this unhappy fate if they had not already attained tenure. For months, we suffered their disappointment with Chan and Jane and then shared their happiness when he found a position at Douglas College, the women's college of Rutgers University. Our friendship, kept alive by correspondence and visits, continued over the years.

When I think of my personal involvement in the movement for racial justice, I often compare my background with Carroll's. He had grown up with direct exposure to discrimination against blacks. I asked him one day whether he thought that I ever, by myself, would have taken the initiative to write such a letter to the school board or to do other controversial things if he had not led me to do so. He was quick to remind me of my concerns about racial and religious prejudice in Baltimore and then told me a story from his high school years:

> I met this older fellow on the street and we got to talking. Somehow, he let me know how much he loved to play the piano whenever he got the chance, which wasn't often. I honestly didn't think twice about his color. Besides, my parents had always treated our colored cook almost like family, except she didn't eat with us, of course. Well, we were seated there together on the piano bench trying out a duet when Mother walked in. You should have seen her face! It was mostly shock, as I remember. She never could be unkind. But her disapproval was clear enough for us to end our session shortly. I suppose, that was the beginning of my sense of social injustice and planted the seed of revolt against it in my mind.

I reminded Carroll about Virgie, who worked for us in Baltimore. She ate with us and was almost like family. At least, she was a close friend of my mother's. She often teased Joe by comparing his color to hers when he had a good summer tan. And I'll never forget how sweet she was on our wedding day. In Indiana, it had been different. Our help in the home was mostly Ball State College girls—all white then—working for their room and board. When we were still very young, we had a white washlady—lady, mind you!

* * *

I loved it when Carroll and I found time to talk together. With all our arguments—and the boys heard a lot of them when they were not too personal—we still found one another's company exciting. I was grateful for Carroll's wonderful sense of humor and was working on my own. He could make me smile, no matter how angry I was, during any dispute when I was hanging on with self righteous stubbornness. He had only to say, with gracious condescension, "You're forgiven." I had never found a rejoinder for that.

* * *

There was, briefly, another member of our family, who influenced our lives deeply. At a Quaker monthly meeting in 1961, Carroll made the offer, subject to my later approval, to help with the housing of a twenty-year-old Yugoslavian refugee until he could establish himself in this country. Assistance with learning English came primarily from the one most available and ready to give it— me. It was a challenging task and a joy as well. As usual, however, it was difficult for me not to become closely involved in the young man's almost overwhelming problems.

It is not surprising that I would describe this involvement best in a poem, but before including it here, I want to say that the story ended well. By the time Grandfather Feagins, whose apartment Andjelko was using, returned from his annual trip to Georgia, our refugee was ready to leave us for a self-supporting job and to apply for citizenship, which he eventually obtained.

OUR YUGOSLAV

Five months ago from camp in Capua
by ship, by crowded train
in sponsored flight
to us
who nearly missed him
in the night;
a name called out—
Andjelko—
gone the fright,
and the anxious face
assumes a cautious
eagerness.

One word remembered
from the tongue of music:
Benvenuto!
Handclasp,

hopeful eyes
before the question:
"Do you speak a little English?"
Shy reply: *Un poco.*
Almost none at all
and no French,
no German.
So we try
the universal speech
of gesture.

Five months of wandering
into at first almost
impenetrable depths
with winding paths
ascending and descending,
marked by signs
in diverse languages
too often misdirecting
when suddenly one day
the signs are English,
English only,
and the shaded thickets
grow less frequent
while a softly filtered light
reveals more often
here and there a clearing;
the eyes of a frightened deer
are suddenly the eyes
of a timid child;
the handclasp has become
a hold upon a teacher's heart
endearing.

Ahead
the light discloses
landmarks grown familiar;
momentary flashes
now portend
the end
of our wandering;
the heart flickers
and the eyes of the child
are gone.

It is good
that in the sixth month
the common path
divides,
the hands unclasp
the heart lets go.
The man walks on
alone.

9

FROM LOCH LOMOND
TO SOUNION

Summer 1963

One aim remained always in the back of my mind: I wanted to travel with Carroll to places I had visited, and many more. The opportunity arrived in 1963, when Mother came to Guilford College to be hostess of the Ragsdale Alumni House. She made it financially possible for us, along with David, to spend that summer in Europe. We planned to have David spend the middle of the three months in the Lycée Jaccard, a boarding school in Switzerland, where he might learn a little French while getting acquainted with boys his own age from all over the world. We tried to persuade Carroll, Jr. to join us, but he had declared his independence upon graduating from high school and did not want to leave his factory job.

It was exciting to pick out a car for rent and possible purchase. After reading aloud to Carroll about the Citroën 2CV in both the *National Geographic* and *Popular Science* magazines, we decided that it sounded by far the most economical, most comfortable, and most fun of all the cars listed in our brochures. I placed an order.

When the three of us sailed on June 2 (after David's whirlwind introduction to New York City) we had four fixed dates: on June eighth, we were expected at Mrs. Zurita's Guest House in London, which offered "hot and cold water laid on"; on June 25, the 2CV would be waiting for us in Paris; on July 7, David's school would begin; and on September 6, we would sail home from Cherbourg. At some time between June 25 and July 7, we wanted to see a Guilford College student, Patricia Miller, who was working near Hanover and planning to spend her junior year in Munich. I was also eager to see Aennchen Kowitz again, to meet her family, and to introduce my own. Apart from these dates, we had no fixed plans. We were going to leave our vacation open to chance encounters while we visited as many cities of our choice as precious time and funds would allow. I was planning to keep my usual journal, which would help me recall everything later.

We rented a car in London and Carroll soon became a good driver on the left side of the road. We drove to Torbay, to see in reality the etching Miss Bussey gave me as a wedding gift, then back through the Midlands toward Edinburgh and Loch Lomond, the farthest north we planned to drive in Scotland.

In Paris, we went by Metro to pick up the Citroën 2CV. We found our new car waiting for us near Versailles. After initial instructions, Carroll drove us, during rush hour and a traffic jam, back to the Hotel des Ecoles, the only one mentioned in both the AAA guide and Frommer's *Europe on Five Dollars a Day.*

I wrote home about our success with Frommer: "[We are] living under $5 a person for room, board, gas and most other expenses. Some of our added expenses run us up to around $20 a day for the three of us. But it looks as if we can average about what we had hoped to. By train or bus, we could not possibly do all we are accomplishing."

I expressed our pleasure in David's company. "He is getting a lot out of this trip. There is a normal amount of friction because of different tastes and because he is obviously a 'third' who tends to vie for attention. But he has rapidly adjusted to the idea of meeting people in a friendly spirit rather than ignoring them, as he started to do." We were also seeing the value of traveling for bonding with our son.

In a letter to Ed Burrows from Lausanne, I described our earlier drive in Germany along the Rhine in our open car, with David photographing a few of the many castles. Later the same day we drove up to the Konigsstuhl high above Heidelberg and then down to the castle, with David standing up the whole way. We had a delightful walk through the courtyard and had a view of the town below at sunset. David remembered my stories of 1937 and remarked, "Mother, you must have some deep feelings—seeing all these things again after so many years!" He can be very perceptive.

The reunion in Munich with Aennchen Kowitz was wonderful. After a coffee hour in the afternoon, Carroll and I returned for a real German "Butterbrot und kalte Schnitte" supper, while David ate out near the hotel and retired early. He had been reading *Mad Magazine*—in French! Rain kept us from seeing much of the city, but we planned to pass through again on our way to Austria, Yugoslavia and Greece.

Before the reunion in Munich, however, we had a good one with Pat Miller. We spent the night at the Herberge, the most economical yet, and in a sylvan setting with air so pure that I had to lie awake breathing it! The director insisted that Pat was everyone's favorite. She looked well and happy. And our visit to the electronics plant the next day removed any doubts about her job there. We met with the owner, who spoke highly of her, of how she arrived punctually every day on her bicycle and how she was taking good advantage of weekends in Hannover, where she had made good friends. She was becoming quite fluent in German.

* * *

In our correspondence with Carroll, Jr. we were bonding differently than with David. It was the first of many times that we would be leaving him at home with some responsibility to us, which he always fulfilled faithfully.

On July 13, I wrote him about a drive in Heidelberg to Blumenstrasse 4. The street was still on the map and we found the old address without any trouble. To my surprise, Pension Hornbeck looked the same as the day I left it. The area in the vicinity of the university had remained unchanged, even though Heidelberg had grown into a much larger town with some very modern sections. Against the yellow brick wall that still enclosed the large villa of the same brick a bicycle was leaning, just as I had often left mine for short intervals. As Carroll slowed to allow me time to recapture my memories, the gate suddenly opened. A tall, dark-haired man came out, followed by a slender youth who clearly resembled him. I grabbed Carroll's arm excitedly and asked him quickly to stop the car. "That man resembles Anna Ceresa's brother . . . And that could be his son." But I did not allow what could easily be fantasy to continue. I suppressed the main question I would ask if it really happened to be Alberto: "Tonino? Has he become the good doctor he was planning to be?" The pair had already started up the hill toward the university and I suggested that we drive on.

Letters home covered most of the main events before our separation from David for the middle month and our drive to Vienna. Our stay there was rich in music. There were waltzes with dinner in the Grinzingerraum of the Ratskeller nearby, opera in the Theatre an der Wien, also nearby, and an organ recital in St. Stephan's Dom, a long walk from our pension. Much of the rest of the time we spent in making arrangements for traveling through Hungary en route to Yugoslavia and Greece.

Inquiring at the American consular service, we were told that the quickest way would be to work through the Austrian Reiseburo. We were, moreover, discouraged from attempting the drive through Hungary. The man helping us even used terms equivalent to washing his hands of the entire business! So we went to the travel office in Vienna and began the long procedure of filling out, in German, forms for Hungary. A very friendly employee, filled with information and savoir faire, supervised the ordeal. She discovered in the process that we had to have our Yugoslavian visa in our passports before the Hungarian visas could be obtained.

We were beginning to worry about our prospective trip. We wondered if the man at the consulate wasn't right, after all. Then we remembered Julia Branson, the Philadelphia Quaker working at the American Friends Service Committee office in Vienna. We had been told to look her up. She might know what we ought to do. So we went to see her. She welcomed us cordially and we had an encouraging half-hour visit. Her attitude was as cheerful as the one at the consulate had been disheartening:

"You shouldn't have any trouble at all. Quakers have not let the wall or the fence keep them from their neighbors anywhere. We're allowed to take relief packages regularly into the East. Someone goes over from here frequently."

"We should have come to you first," I declared. "You don't know how relieved this makes us feel. They told us at the consulate that no one was going into Hungary now. But, actually, we've found friendly people everywhere."

"Well, you're discovering for yourselves what you often hear but don't quite comprehend without the experience. Human beings are basically alike everywhere."

Carroll and I left with our minds clear and our hopes high. Still, as we approached the Hungarian border two days later, we could not help but feel a little apprehensive—mostly because of the reactions of other persons who heard we were driving through. But everything went smoothly. At Shopron, we were let in after a few formalities. We lacked some triplicate form concerning money and that held us up. There was a perfunctory search of the car and suitcases—the first time we opened a suitcase at any border—but the officials appeared to be making a show of the required routine without being very serious about the search. Everyone was polite. I, "keeper of the exchequer," exchanged exactly four dollars out of my seven dollars in bills, although I was advised at the window to cash a ten-dollar check. With a change purse already fat with francs (both kinds), schillings, marks and three lira, I did not care to have any Hungarian change left over.

There was indication of an approaching fair, and flags of many nations, including the United States, were on display. Once over the border, we felt alone and at liberty in the 2CV, with no traffic in sight. We soon saw that the roads were the most clearly marked of any we had encountered—perhaps with the intention of seeing us through the country as quickly as possible and without unnecessary detours. After all, we did have only a *Durchreise* (one-day) pass.

On both sides were rich, irrigated, and well-cultivated farmlands, stretching for miles, and large areas of the same crops. There were no scattered farmhouses, the fields apparently being worked in common by the people, who dwelt in villages at distant intervals. The work in the fields was being done with the most primitive tools, such as wooden pitchforks made from forks of trees. There was little sign of mechanized farming.

The roads we saw were really lovely, many of them reminiscent of those in Northern France, bordered by large trees or newly planted saplings. Although the main road was fair, it was inferior to those of Austria, and the villages we were passing looked poor. Wherever children were working near the road, they turned excitedly to greet us—almost frantic in their enthusiasm.

Close to the border, we had been stopped twice by guards, as our map showed we would be, the second time being asked to show our papers. We met few vehicles: motorcycles, bicycles, and horse-drawn wagons, most without rubber tires, and almost no passenger cars. There were some Austrian cars and, in or near towns, some old-model foreign cars bearing native plates, and no modern American cars at all. We felt as though we were the only persons from America in Hungary that day.

We enjoyed the ride along the Danube and, at several points, could see Czechoslovakia across the way. Because a large distributer was out of gas and waiting for the afternoon delivery, we were forced to buy special gas coupons to use at a small gas station, where dealers could not accept cash.

Budapest's beautiful past was still evident in its historical structures. We were struck, however, by the struggle to revive after the devastations of war and revolt. We saw here, for the first time, the use of heavy timber as scaffolding instead of steel, which seemed totally lacking.

As we parked on a centrally located square near the Danube, we were immediately surrounded by curious citizens and their children, poking their heads into and around the car. We were in the process of pantomiming our desire for lunch, when we were joined by a middle-aged woman with a blonde child walking by her side and a brunette, curly-headed baby girl of perhaps eight months sitting serenely, in utter and beautiful nakedness, in a handsome perambulator. The woman turned out to be the Hungarian nursemaid of children of a German family from whom she had learned enough of the language to communicate well with me. She assured us and the others around us that the place on the square that the natives were suggesting for lunch was expensive and that she would direct us to a nice but less expensive restaurant. Carroll and I were easier to persuade than those gathered around us, but the little group reluctantly turned us over to the maid. They relayed the message that the car should be left locked and one of them, who lived within view, would keep an eye on it.

What a sight we must have presented: perambulator with naked baby leading the way, being pushed by nurse with barefoot, blonde girl following, and, finally, the two strangers hurrying to keep up! The woman was most kind, obviously going out of her way to lead us to what turned out to be a respectable hotel and restaurant with reasonable prices. German was spoken there, too, so that we could easily order what we wanted from several inviting items on the menu.

We found our 2CV just as we had parked it. Before leaving, we bought postcards and, from the shopkeeper, I learned the two phrases I intended to learn in every foreign country: *koszonom* (thank you) and *viszontlatasra* (auf Wiedersehen). This came about after the shopkeeper had shown us a picture of her friends in Oklahoma!

The afternoon went by rapidly, with much hand waving to children along the way. Only as we approached the Yugoslavian border did we see one area where there were some scattered farmhouses with smaller plots of cultivated land. We passed an army convoy shortly before the border, but we saw little evidence of propaganda, like pictures and slogans, only red stars at police stations and other civic buildings plus the hammer and sickle on modest monuments here and there.

At the border, we received polite treatment. We had to leave the car (as we had at Shopron), but the wait for our documents to be examined proved to be short and pleasant. There was a quick glance into the car but luggage was not checked here or across the border. Nor was there any inquiry about money, to my relief, for I still had a few dollars in undeclared bills.

It seemed appropriate that we should spend our first night in Novi Sad—New Garden—a favorite name for Quaker meetings. We were there, primarily, to look up Andjelko's brother, but when we finally found his apartment, he was not at home. We left a note from Andjelko and our regrets.

The rest of this chapter could be devoted to the subject of Yugoslavian roads: the beautiful local color on each side, including a bikini-clad beauty strolling alone; the international signs (especially the "!") appearing too often after the designated hazard had been met; and the deep potholes, challenging the 2CV's tires and suspension.

There is one incident concerning this subject so impressive that it caused me to write about it as it happened:

Between Jajce & Sarajevo
3:00 P.M. July 22

We are with a large group of people watching a lone hero on a bulldozer rebuild a road that has just been partly washed out by a stream, swollen by recent rains and pouring down the mountainside, bringing with its gushing large boulders to block the narrow ledge on its way to the valley far below. Near us is an elderly woman holding her Turkish trousers up out of the mud. The majority of the spectators—in several varieties of dress and speech representing different nationalities—are crowded as close to the bulldozer as possible, crying out with a mixture of fear and delight as they have to scramble from time to time for safety.

A couple of brave souls just waded by us on a motorcycle, passing the long line of parked cars near the abyss. Our little "deux-chevaux" is fourth in line to attempt the crossing of the brand new road—whenever it is completed. Two large buses are awaiting their turn further along the line. We are followed directly by another 2CV, owned by a genuine Frenchman and his wife. (We are often taken for French because of our car.)

With my phrase book I managed to question a native: "Will we go tonight?" I used *Hoce li ovo pismo otici veceras?* (indicating) the four of us who were waiting. (*Ovo pismo* means "this letter.") My Yugoslav friend understood and assured me "This very night."

I also asked "*Gde jesmo?*" and was shown on our map exactly where we were.

Now I am sitting in the car and can see well enough that minor (I hope!) engine trouble has halted the proceedings. Carroll is standing in a front-row position.

And now the bulldozer is at work again.

3:35

We've made it!

Carroll had occasion later to discuss this subject with a young couple crossing from Igoumenitsa, Greece, by ship-ferry to Brindisi, Italy.

"But I'll have to say this," he told his new acquaintances, "Mary and I have those roads to thank for our lives. She was determined to follow the journey of Rebecca West, described in her book, *Black Lamb and Gray Falcon*. If we had stayed one more night to drive around Lake Ohrid, à la Rebecca West, we'd have still been in Skoplje as planned . . . and for the earthquake!

Our providential escape from the earthquake and the reunion with David in Rome were the two most dramatic events of the summer.

A letter to Ed from Carroll was mailed on July 31 from Athens, shortly after we had sent a cablegram. It explained how we had spent the night of the twenty-fourth in Skoplje, in the very hotel (the *Macedonia*) which was flattened less than twenty-four hours after our departure.

(There was also an important request that Carroll had to make of Ed. Finances seemed to be doing well and we were still thinking of buying the car and bringing it home with us. But, just in case, Carroll was enclosing a check for eight hundred dollars for Ed to cash and send to us by American Express in Paris by August 25.

We arrived in Rome on Sunday. And we expected David the next day at the earliest. After settling in at a convent listed in the back of Frommer under "Readers' Choices," we drove to the Termini to check on train schedules for possible arrival times in the morning. We hoped to have word from David at the American Express in the morning, since nothing had arrived at Athens before we left.

He arrived earlier than we were expecting him to. I recall all my apprehension about this, and then on Monday, the harrowing experiences at the railroad station and American Express and telephone office (long distance to Lausanne without success—trying to find the time-of-arrival of David's train). Finally, we received notice (in Italian) on our second trip to the American Express, that our son could be found in the American Consulate. We dashed there by taxi, to find that he had been well cared for during the night and was either at the railroad station or at the YMCA. After rushing back by taxi, we had him paged at the station. No response. Finally, Carroll found him by chance. David had not heard the paging because he was outside having a snack.

I can never forget how he looked, tired and sweaty, lugging his heavy suitcase with clothes sticking out one end, and holding his tennis racket and overcoat with one arm. He had packed his dirty clothes in with his clean ones. We paid a visit to the consulate, to thank Ms. Arthur for her assistance and to let her "see David happy." That kind secretary had sent out for a copy of Frommer and phoned every hotel that was recommended under Rome, but neither David nor she had noticed the section in the back. If they had, they would have found the convent, which proved to be a restful place to stay after the hectic but happy reunion, and a great place to wash clothes.

Our large scrapbook holds the record of our drive from Rome by the sea-road to Pisa, to Florence, back to Pisa and along the Italian Riviera, over to Milan, Venice and Trieste, then down the Dalmation Coast to Zadar. (We wanted to give David a taste of Yugoslavia as well as to spread out our dwindling funds more economically. I had discovered we would run out of money if we spent too much of our remaining time in more expensive countries.) As it turned out, the drive from Zadar, where we stayed several days, to Split and back was one of the most interesting. But, more exciting, was our attempt to enter Austria at the Loibl Pass only to find that our little 2CV could not make the steep grade. It was clear why a tunnel was under construction there! We had to turn around and use the recommended pass to Klagenfurt.

During my junior year in Germany, I had never visited Berlin. So, after a brief visit to Passau and Nurenberg, we drove by the corridor from Hof to West Berlin. We managed our visit from there to East Germany without much difficulty. We felt free to drive where we pleased and to see what we wished until we decided to take a look at the airport. This was "verboten." The fact of the wall plus the fact that West Berliners could not enter with the same freedom as tourists made us feel an air of oppression that we could not actually see. We did see more propaganda everywhere than in West Berlin, however.

Back in West Germany, we visited Luebeck, where we met Gertrude Victorius's relatives in their ancestral home. From there we drove to Hoorn and elsewhere in Holland and Belgium, to the final lap of our summer tour. This took us to Paris by way of Peronne. Our financial status was not good! My journal has a record of our last days:

August 31

Peronne en route to Paris. Peronne was not bad— shoddy, but clean at least—and it enabled us to eat dinner and have three cups of morning coffee in addition to our night's lodging. We had cashed our last traveler's check; gas, bed and board left us with exactly 20 centimes when we set out in the rain for Paris.

We arrived without a hitch at around 10:30. We found a parking place near the side entrance of the American Express (opposite the Opera House) and went in to get the eagerly anticipated and absolutely necessary check from Ed and the bank. It was there. We made application for reservations on train coach from NYC to Greensboro, drove to the Hotel Central, went to our favorite Rotisserie du Pantheon for noonday dinner and just in time to say farewell to our favorite waitress before the restaurant closed for vacation.

Having learned, much to his surprise, that he would pay for the car upon its delivery in the USA, where he would also receive title for it, Carroll planned to drive it to Le Havre while David and I waited at Cherbourg. He joined us after what seemed to us a long day of waiting and we prepared for debarkation on the following day.

The crossing was rough—a northern route to escape the worst of a storm. Only after our arrival did we discover that the captain had sighted an iceberg, which explained the frequent overpasses of a navy plane sent to observe and help out if necessary. (There was an article in the *New York Times* telling of the danger and the preparation for possible "seeding" from the plane to break up the iceberg.)

Eager to get home, after less than an hour in customs, the three of us rode to Penn Station and changed the reservations made at Paris to the afternoon Southerner (5:45) and telephoned Ed. He met us at 2:15 A.M. along with Carroll, Jr. and Granddaddy Feagins. Grandmother Brown would be back from a visit on the following day.

Ed often took delight in describing the return of the tourists. "They looked utterly exhausted—laden with suitcases and net bags stuffed to the limit with everything from tennis racket to wooden shoes." Arriving at such an early hour had not improved our tired appearance.

It had been a never-to-be-forgotten summer. It would prove to be the only carefree "family" jaunt that Carroll and I would make to Europe—carefree, of course, only if you do not count the near catastrophe in Skoplje and the anxious hours before our reunion with David in the Termini at Rome.

My mother, Suzette Lavonne Willcutts.

ABOVE: *Mary Ellen reading at an early age.*

BELOW: *With my brother David on our front porch, 812 W. North Street, Muncie, Indiana.*

Mary Ellen and David in Chinese costumes brought from China by Uncle Mort Willcutts.

ABOVE: *On my "trusty" bike in Frau Nassauer's garden in Heidelberg, July 1937.*

BELOW: *Brother Joe in Bavarian outfit.*

LEFT: *Frau Blumtritt with son Eberhard in Reisach bei Oberaudorf, 1937.*
RIGHT: *Frau Lüttgens, our* Hausmutter, *Kaulbach Strasse, 69, Munich.*

*Aennchen Malmann von Ameluxen,
Munich friend, 1937–1938, to become
lifetime friend.*

Fasching *party at the Ruoff's, Bill Sherwood and I as Chinese (I am looking at him in 2nd row and Kay Shedd is directly behind him).*

Float in Fasching *parade.*

ABOVE: Carroll Feagins as accompanist for Duke Glee Club.

BELOW: *September 10, 1941, Wedding Reception at home on Wakefield Road in Baltimore. With bride and groom on right and best man (Tom Cottingham) and maid of honor (Jean Lane) on left. The Presbyterian minister between the couples, Carroll's father at right. Back row left to right are organist (Tom Curtis), soloist (Jake Wagoner), ushers (Wallace Scherer and Joe Loftis).*

10

NEW CHALLENGES

1963–1965

Soon after our return from the European trip of the summer of 1963, Mother devised a plan that would effectively negate repayment of her loan that had made it possible. During that summer, she had decided to give up her position as hostess at the alumni house. It was beginning to be too demanding for even her energies. At the same time, Grandfather Feagins fell in love with a friend of many years, who had lost her husband shortly before Ruby died. He moved to Georgia to marry her and share her home. The Grandparents' Apartment was made available for Grandmother Brown. That was the time for her to implement her idea of paying us a small monthly rent "on paper" until the amount of the loan was reached. She promptly dismissed our immediate protests, obviously pleased with her plan as if she had just pulled off a surprise birthday party for a favorite child.

I was not really so surprised. I was used to Mother's ability to perform a generous act while making the recipient feel like the one to whom she was indebted. So I persuaded Carroll to abide by the new agreement and to accept the adventures of our wonderful summer as a gift of large proportions. The classroom was now a livelier place for me since I had so much that was new to draw on. David had benefitted from his experience at the Lycée Jaccard and was doing better in school. Carroll, Jr. had interrupted his factory work to try college, only to give it up immediately. He was less settled, but I was learning how to let go of him—to let him find himself.

At this same time, the college was changing presidents. Clyde Milner was retiring and Grimsley Hobbs, a former student of Carroll's, had risen high enough in his academic field to be seriously considered as the successor. The fact that he was also the grandson of the first president of the college added to his suitability and to general interest in him. During their two years at Guilford, he and his wife, Lois Ann, had been capable and likeable young parents as well as excellent students. We encouraged and looked forward to their coming in this new administrative role.

Then, there arrived a letter to Carroll from the American Friends Service Committee asking him to consider a two-year term as a leader in its overseas program Quaker International Conferences and Seminars in South and Southeast Asia—CONSEM for short. It was directed by two leaders, whose terms of service were for two years, arranged so that an annual replacement arrived to overlap the second year of the remaining director. This had come about partly as a result of a casual comment Carroll had made the year before. We had gone around to say goodbye to our friends Warren and Helen Ashby as they prepared to leave for Philadelphia to begin orientation for his AFSC CONSEM appointment as co-leader. As we were leaving, Carroll called out, "Send for me for your second year." So Carroll was to join Warren for his second year and to remain to be joined by someone else for the following year.

CONSEM was an ambitious program, almost overwhelming in its breadth, covering an area from Afghanistan and Pakistan to the Philippines. It meant traveling about, meeting strategic persons who could suggest names of participants and places of gatherings, and then actually conducting the three types of international programs: conferences for diplomats, seminars for university students, and conferences for young Asian leaders. The many details would be outlined during a week of orientation, should Carroll be interested in the post. It was volunteer service, with no remuneration outside of expenses of the co-director and any family members who accompanied him.

It sounded exciting, although I had to confess to Carroll, I had never thought of serving in India. I had dreamed of doing what the Newlins had done, managing the Friends Center in Geneva . . . or something like that. I was probably thinking of being able to use my French and German. But this would be his job. I would just be going along as a supportive wife. Excitement and caution vied with each other in my mind.

The thought of doing something positive for international understanding and peace—something more direct, perhaps, than teaching, sounded challenging to Carroll. His only concern was whether he could do a good job. I felt certain that he could. However, two years would be a long time to be away from our jobs at Guilford. Still, David was at a good place for a break. He could stand a year or so between high school and college—especially since we started him a year early at Page Private School. He was ready then for first grade, but we were not so sure that he had matured enough to take further study seriously right now. He certainly did get a lot out of travel and the Lycée Jaccard. Living in India would be an education in itself. I had one important question. Could we get Carroll, Jr. to go along with us? Carroll remarked that since this son had given up a job to try college and then left before classes even started, his interest now was to get back into another well-paying job. He was old enough to look after himself and could look in on my mother while we were gone. I knew, then, that Carroll had made up our minds to go.

* * *

Together we flew with sun westward flame-feathered skies
from San Francisco to Honolulu and one day dropped
like a knitter's stitch before Tokyo . . .

In order to familiarize Carroll with a part of the extensive program he would be co-directing, the home office in charge of CONSEM sent us to India by way of Japan, where we would learn more about the AFSC international programs. There was a two-week orientation at AFSC headquarters in Philadelphia. Then we flew to Tokyo, by way of Chicago, San Francisco and Honolulu, where we would have an overnight rest.

Chan and Jane Ives drove from their home in Kingston, New Jersey, to have lunch with us at the airport and see us off from Philadelphia. I was happy for the layover of several hours in San Francisco. It gave Mort and Marie, now living on Belvedere Island, enough time to meet us at the airport for a whirlwind reunion.

"Watch out for the amoeba!" warned Uncle Mort, with his stern doctor's voice. "It's not the 'bugs' that are so bad—it's the damned 'eggs.' Some people just can't get rid of them . . . ever."

Somehow, those words caused me to shudder. Were they at all

prophetic? They seemed unusually ominous after a similar warning from Frank Graham. We had stopped to talk briefly to him in his office during a visit to the United Nations, arranged as part of our orientation program. He had emphasized the importance of using only boiled water. "Some forget this when it comes to cleaning their teeth. See that you always use boiled water . . . even for your toothbrush! Buy yourselves two large teakettles and boil enough for the whole day." Those had been his farewell words.

In Japan, we were greeted by members of the Friends Center and Helen Barns. Helen had returned as soon as possible after the war to Yokohama, where she was again teaching at Seibi Gakuen. She was happy to be back at this school after the years of interruption by war. She had come by train to join the welcoming party from the Center, where we would be staying. She announced enthusiastically that she had already arranged with our local hosts for us to use part of our free time to visit her bungalow on the grounds of the school.

Friends Center was an attractive, Western-style house, sharing a compound with a Quaker meeting house, one of only two in Tokyo. David was pleased to be given the single Japanese room, on the ground floor. Carroll and I were led to small, adjoining rooms upstairs. During supper, we were given an outline of the program planned for us. It included a two-day stay with international workers at a leper colony on the outskirts of Tokyo and a long weekend in a village on Mt. Bondai. We would be participating in international seminars and work camps.

During the first night, I was awakened by rattling windows; then I noticed that my bed was shaking. I ran into Carroll's room and found him awake, too. Since the activity was over quickly, I returned to my bed and to sleep. At breakfast, as Carroll began to ask the question, Fumiko Miho, hostess at the Center, smiled in anticipation and said, "Yes. I know what you are going to ask. A little introductory quake was planned as part of your orientation."

"An earthquake? I didn't feel anything!" David was disappointed that his deep sleep, on futon and on tatami floor, had caused him to miss the excitement.

We had arrived on Sunday, July 11, 1965. Monday was a real holiday. During the day there was a visit to the Ginza and attendance at a kabuki theater. In the evening there was a sukiyaki dinner in farewell to the Wilsons, who were returning to the USA after three years at the Center. Tuesday and Wednesday were likewise not workdays.

Early on Thursday morning, as I lay in bed, a poem begun in Honolulu continued to form in my mind. Reaching for my journal and pencil, I began to describe hastily the memories of the past two days:

> from Tokyo to Kyoto by Tokaido Express
> —"the way facing the eastern ocean"—
> windows flashing by Hiroshige's stations
> stereoptical merging of present and past
> suspended in color prints and poetry . . .
> framing the intuited seasons.

It was an incredibly fast ride. In Kyoto, we had been met by the mother of Shizue Mori, a Japanese graduate of Guilford. That friendly lady had arranged a beautiful introduction to the former capital city, a night in a dormitory of the new university, and a side-trip to the old capital Nara. She also took us to our first Japanese restaurant.

Back in Tokyo on Wednesday night, we were housed in a hotel near the Olympic Stadium. Perhaps the most spectacular sight was the Ginza at night. Never before had we seen such elaborate neon signs. The colors and complexity of design were marvelous and seemed almost endless in variety. Accompanying this visual delight was the sensation of multitudes of people in the streets, the sound of flapping sandals and the feeling of being overtaken by throngs behind us as we plied our way through throngs ahead. Yet, many went out of their way to be friendly and helpful when we three visitors appeared to be lost.

On the following Sunday, Helen came to attend Friends meeting for worship and to take the three of us by train to Yokohama. In the middle of the afternoon, David was thrilled to experience his first earthquake. If anything, it was a bit more significant than the one he had missed the preceding Sunday night. Nevertheless, both were very minor, Helen assured us, and declared that she hoped David would be satisfied with his one experience.

Before she accompanied us, in the early evening, back to Tokyo, she secured our promise to spend our final Japanese days with her. Those responsible for our program had agreed to let Helen see Carroll off to Saigon on the twenty-ninth and David and me off to Delhi two days later.

The remainder of the three-week visit to Japan was an introduction to international programs of the American Friends Service Committee and the Friends Service Council of London. A day and a night at the leprosarium educated us in the progress that had been made in developing humanitarian ways of enabling sufferers of the disease to rebuild constructive lives with self-esteem. We were amazed at the size and productivity of the village and the success of treatment of virulent cases. Leprosy could now be arrested and made non-communicable so that patients could return to their families. The main industry of the village was the manufacture of custom-built shoes for those whose feet were deformed by the disease.

Carroll and David joined the male members of an international group of work campers, while I joined the women for our overnight stay in temporary sleeping quarters at a school there. The next day, we joined the workers in building a new path through one of the large gardens that helped make the village self-sufficient. I was surprised at how quickly I grew accustomed to men and women whose faces and limbs had been ravaged and eroded before treatment and cure, mingling with healthy children of all ages.

David made some good friends from among the young internationals. He attended seminars of his choosing, while Carroll and I did the same. It was an eye-opening experience for David to find young people presenting points of view in opposition to what he was accustomed to hear from his peer group, particularly in respect to the involvement of the United States in Vietnam. It was not entirely new to him; we had, after all, let our own views be known to both sons and had tried to make clear that patriotism demanded constructive criticism of one's government. To hear criticism of the United States coming from young people of Japan, India, Holland, or elsewhere aroused in him a defensive spirit; at the same time, he had to recognize the validity of many of their statements.

Tayeko Yamanouchi, who helped to direct international programs in the East, was the chief source of inspiration and guidance for us in Tokyo. Widowed during the war with China, she had become a convinced Friend, was active with the Friends World Committee for Consultation, and was to have a marked influence on my thinking. She planned what turned out to be the most memorable event in connection with our pre-India orientation in the East. This was the trip to Mt. Bondai. Because train travel was so crowded that we would have to be at the station at 7:00 A.M. for a 9:00 A.M. departure, Tayeko made reservations for us at a typical Japanese inn near the station. Here we would have authentic sleeping arrangements, with futon, kimono, gratis toothbrush, soap and towel, tea in our room, authentic bathroom facilities, and authentic supper and break-fast!

We had never quite been able to believe the stories we had read about the necessity for "pushers"—employed, literally, to push passengers onto the overcrowded trains of Tokyo. But, after sitting for two hours on the platform we joined the hundreds who had to be pushed onto the train and pointed in the direction of our reserved seats! There we spent a long day, with a break for a late lunch, beautifully packed in little jars and paper packages, and then a short nap. We hated to miss any of the colorful landscapes and villages the train was passing through. It slowly climbed to the hill country and, finally, to near the top of Mt. Bondai. A rickety bus took us to Fukushima, the village where another international work camp was located. This was the area given to Japanese veterans of World War II and their families, and it was a most unlikely spot for farming. Indeed, we were told, this was the highest spot in the world where rice was grown. The project in which we were to participate was helping to build a road that would enable the farmers to get their produce more easily to markets below.

For two days, we shared meals, pushed wheelbarrows, smoothed dirt, showered with a hose from a barrel full of scarcely warmed water above our heads, played getting-acquainted games, and sang songs before bedtime. An early morning climb to the village's small temple would have made the long trip worth our while, even without the congeniality of this variegated group of people drawn close together for a few weeks in a common cause.

On Wednesday, the twenty-eighth, we returned to Yokohama and celebrated Carroll's birthday with Helen. We were invited for "tea ceremony" at the home of her friend, Kikue, and to meet Kikue's father, a well-known art collector and editor. David was excused early to take the local train to the city, to explore a little on his own. It seemed like a good idea until midnight arrived without his return. As we became anxious, Helen assured us that we had no cause for alarm. We bravely hid our growing concern as we continued to converse on different subjects, but we were greatly relieved when, shortly before one o'clock, we heard David's hurried steps. He reported to us excitedly of the wrestling match he had stopped to watch. When he saw our concern, he reminded us that he was seventeen years old—old enough to look after himself. We had to agree and were pleased that he had managed this adventure on his own.

The next day, Carroll was scheduled to meet an American Friends Service Committee representative in Saigon. If I had known that he would be driven about that city on the back of a motorcycle and introduced to what would seem to me to be perilous situations, I would have been more anxious about the days ahead. But I did not allow any apprehensions or sadness over our brief parting to dampen his enthusiasm for the adventures he anticipated. Helen helped David and me see him off on Air France and then prepare for our own departure, two days later, for Delhi.

11
INDIA
1965

I was reading in *Time* magazine about air skirmishes over Saigon when the pilot announced that we were flying high above Vietnam. I thought of Carroll. David was thinking of his dad, too, and wondering what he was doing right then, down there in the midst of everything. We would be coming down in Rangoon—one adventure that Carroll would miss because he would be flying by way of Bangkok.

We had a smooth landing in Rangoon. It was too bad we could not leave the airport. The only glimpses we had of Burma were of the clean-up crew in the large waiting room, with its colorful murals, and a few temples rapidly disappearing at take-off.

Stepping out of the plane in Delhi's night air was like stepping out of an air-conditioned room into a sauna. This simile I could only imagine, for I had not yet experienced a sauna outside of literature. I was not imagining, however, the sweet smell of dung smoke pervading the air, although I could identify it only from Bradford Smith's description in his *Portrait of India*. Jane Ives had sent this book to me as soon as she heard we were coming to India. I clutched my two handbags (one filled with gamma globulin and disposable needles to be hand-delivered to Quaker House for a few persons who had been exposed to hepatitis) and held onto David's arm. Both of us were too overwhelmed for words. Faded colors, exotic smells, the din of chattering and shouting voices came at us from all sides, as we moved in silence across the field to the airport terminal building. In all the crowds, there was no sign of a familiar face. We allowed ourselves to be pushed through customs—much quicker, I learned many months later, than we should have been. Did we have any unaccompanied baggage? Well . . . yes, but those footlockers had arrived weeks earlier and had already been picked up, we were certain, by Warren Ashby. No one offered us any declaration papers to fill out on this subject. We were happy to be through so quickly.

Still, there was no one there to meet us. So we went to a desk and inquired for any messages. None. We showed a man the address and phone number of the Ashbys, and he was kind enough to place the call. Helen's voice sounded far away. She hastily apologized: Warren was out of town and she had been given the wrong time. She would send Devendra in a taxi to get us right away. "Just wait there a few more minutes."

Two shabbily dressed bearers had already grabbed our suitcases in spite of our objections. We were used to handling our own luggage when it was at all manageable. But the two friendly fellows waited with us before the main entrance until Devendra arrived. This handsome young Indian was on Warren's staff at Quaker House, where the CONSEM program office was located along with the Quaker International Affairs representative. It soon became clear that he had become the Ashbys' main local program assistant and a congenial companion—very much at home in their family. He had high hopes, too, of rising in rank in the service of the AFSC.

Helen met us in the lighted courtyard of the modern, recently built home in Defense Colony, New Delhi. She led us through a spacious living room to the bedroom we would be using. We had our first sight of a *charpoy,* the narrow "string" cot that waited for David along the far wall. A double bed would be shared by Carroll and me if Warren and Helen did not succeed in helping me to find housing before his arrival.

As Helen told us of her work at Lady Irwin's school, I felt a little envious of her. A long talk with Nora, personnel director of the program, had impressed upon me that I was to have one duty only—to make a good home for Carroll and David and to manage the household affairs, including some entertaining. In short, I was to keep the family healthy and happy. There had been some complaints from the Indian government about spouses of program workers who were taking jobs away from unemployed natives. This did not really apply to Helen, however. She was doing some teaching that could be done only by a person with her specialized training and experience. In fact, she was equipping native students to do her work in future. But, in any case, I had been given my "orders." Furthermore, I began to sense, already, that the job outlined for me was challenging enough to keep me busy.

We found an apartment, in Jor Bagh, in New Delhi, not far from where the Quaker Center in Old Delhi was soon to be relocated. Friends meetings and Carroll's office would be within walking distance. It was a second-floor apartment and included the roof.

I was estimating our living expenses to be somewhat below the level of the Ashbys' and somewhat above the level of our predecessors, the Johnsons. The wife of Stan Johnson had grown up in India, could ride her bicycle to and from market, and knew how to bargain with local tradespeople. For a while, my greatest challenge was to learn how to achieve an acceptable style of living that would justify the expense account I would be presenting to the AFSC. It was our first experience at receiving a salary that would be determined by our conscience! And we had no savings of our own to draw upon.

Just as we had been given an allowance for necessary purchases at Sears before leaving the United States, we were now expected to set an allowance for furnishing the modest apartment. First, however, we felt obliged to use whatever we could of the furnishings left behind by the Johnsons. We bought a new bed for David, but Carroll and I thought sleeping on Indian *palangs* (cots) would be fun, for a while at least, and never replaced them. The extras would be needed for overnight guests.

The living/dining area was a spacious rectangle separated by the vestibule and hallway from the bedrooms. It would have to serve as a guest bedroom as well. The two bedrooms were separated by a large bathroom and an air vent that connected the rooms near the ceiling. This was the only way that David could receive benefit from our air conditioner, in the front bedroom; it was also the way his dad and mother later discovered that he had taken up smoking to alleviate his temporary homesickness. David had his own bathroom, off the back porch and across from the kitchen, but was so disappointed that it was Turkish style (already experienced, once in Reims and several times in Yugoslavia), that we asked our landlord to convert it to Western style. He did this without adding to the 800 rupees rent per month because he knew it would increase the value for future tenants.

The small kitchen was off the back porch. From this, we could see the broad alleyway and observe the activities of families across from us. We could watch them in their kitchens, on their porches, and in one garage where a servant and his family lived and worked and often cooked meals outside on a small brazier. We watched, also, as emaciated cows, and sometimes human beings, came to search the community "disposal"—an empty square made of cinderblock, where debris was burned periodically. Once I caught sight of a young boy walking down the alley. I recognized his loud chanting to be that which I had been hearing frequently of early mornings. Upon inquiry, I learned that he was going to a little temple a few blocks away, where he regularly served.

On the front of the apartment there was a sheltered balcony, from which I could watch servants trim and sweep the front lawn or could speak to the young wife sitting below in the sun drying her long and richly highlighted black hair. Best of all, I loved to spend hours on the roof, in one of the wicker chairs placed close to the front ledge so as to provide a spectator's paradise. There I might see a show by a snake charmer or, once, a dance recital by a seven- or eight-year-old girl accompanied by her brother with his drum. On the roof, I coveted for myself the barsati, the three-sided room for a servant. I liked hanging the few articles of clothing that I sometimes washed between the weekly visits of the dhobi, the laundryman shared with the Ashbys and, most likely, others.

It did not take us long to get used to sharing our home with inhabitants who seemed to belong: geckos, lizards who had staked out their respective claims on the ceiling and walls, and a colony of harmless ants that marched in a continuous column from the sideboard to the wall of the porch and the kitchen, where it disappeared into a crack to reappear just behind the sideboard. Since all foods not in the refrigerator were kept in tightly covered cans or boxes, the ants seemed to be marching only for exercise. I drew the line at flies or roaches.

Getting settled took several weeks. We had moved to 200 Jor Bagh on the ninth of August, four days after Carroll's arrival from Saigon by way of Bangkok. For a while, Helen took pleasure in accompanying me on shopping tours. We went by taxi, usually with a Sikh driver, and it was not long before I knew my way around by myself. Never having been one to enjoy shopping, I was astonished at the satisfaction I found in browsing with Helen through the variety of shops at Connaught Place in New Delhi. Even more interesting was the historic street in Old Delhi called Chandni Chowk, "Moonlight Crossing" or, since *chandni* means both moon and silver, "Street of Silver." I rambled along it for hours, poking my nose into all sorts of savory and unsavory little shops. I stared curiously at the great variety of rare art objects, ivoryware, woodcarving, jewelry, embroidery and perfumery, being displayed. They were handled by craftsmen and merchants in the greatest variety of dress or undress that I could have imagined.

With the help of Melissa Asherbranner, the daughter of the Peace Corps director, and Ann Ashby, David likewise became familiar with the city. He had only a few weeks for this complete freedom before he entered St. Stephen's, a part of the University of Delhi. Carroll and I were amused by his being accepted as a "casual" student, the term for one who would not be taking final exams for a degree.

Carroll, himself, was busy getting acquainted with the office and with the job description that Warren Ashby had outlined for the new co-director. For several weeks, this meant a daily trip by taxi to Old Delhi. After that, he had a walk of only a few blocks to the Quaker House relocated in Jor Bagh.

* * *

Michael, son of Ashby's cook, Lawrence, had come to live in the barsati. Under the tutelage of his father, he was trying out his first job as cook. Along with him, he had brought Raghubir (Ragbeer), who combined the services of sweeper and bearer. Michael, like all members of Lawrence's family, was a Christian from a line, he claimed, that stretched back to the earliest followers of Jesus. The apostle Thomas, himself, had come to Malabar and brought the gospel to the Indians long before Francis Xavier in the sixteenth century and Protestants even later. Raghubir was a Hindu and a *Harijan*. He gave me my first concrete evidence that some progress was being made in India, in this largest attempt at democracy—largest, that is, in respect to the extensive and variegated population under one government. In spite of his inherited caste, the lowest, the untouchable, he had received enough education to be able to read and write a little and had picked up enough English to communicate satisfactorily with me.

Raghubir also gave us an opportunity that I often remembered later, especially at Christmas. He provided an occasion that brought us close to the spirit of Christmas in the month of September. He invited us to his home to share in his family's celebration of Lord

Krishna's birthday. This aspect of Hinduism has some similarities with the Christian religion, one of the most striking being the worship of God incarnate in the form of a baby and as a growing child. The birthday of Lord Krishna was being celebrated in this very humble home and in the temple yard, where a pageant was to be held later on that night. At nightfall, we left, feeling honored that we had been invited into the home of this lowly caste.

The fact that Raghubir could understand English was to become very important soon, when Michael proved to be unreliable and otherwise disappointing both to us and to his father. Michael brought a pretty young "divorcee" (who was not yet legally free) to share the barsati, much to Lawrence's disapproval. For this and other reasons, he eventually had to be discharged. Raghubir became our only servant, elevated in rank and salary to fulfill the duties of cook, bearer, or errand-runner, and sweeper. Since the cook did the shopping, I was happy to discover that Raghubir was much more careful with accounting than Michael. The latter had calculated sometimes in old "annas," sometimes in new coinage—depending on the advantage to his own private purchases. In Raghubir's accounting of expenditures, I began to see a clear agreement with local market prices, which I myself had periodically checked and found wanting in Michael's case.

Raghubir stayed on for as long as we remained in Delhi. Since he lived with the family of his widowed mother in Sunlight Colony, I became accustomed to his early morning greeting when he let himself in with his own key. As he walked past the thinly curtained window of our bedroom, he never failed to say cheerfully, "Good morning, sir." He continued to address me with "sir" even after I had explained that this term was reserved for the masculine gender. The English phrase, which he had learned by rote, was too indelibly fixed in his mind.

* * *

On Monday, September 6, we heard our first news of the breaking out of hostilities between India and Pakistan. The news was not entirely unexpected. There had been quiet threats of conflict since early August, but the general public and foreign visitors had had only signs of a possible crisis. Now, the stacks of bricks that had been placed strategically along the road to the Safdarjang airport, visible from our front balcony, took on significance. Workmen appeared who quickly used these bricks to line the deep ditch on the side of the road.

On Tuesday, in the midst of all the excitement, Howard Hinshaw arrived with his friend Al, sooner than expected. Howard was a recent graduate of Guilford who was also a member of New Garden Meeting. He had been doing volunteer work in Kenya. They were just in time to join us for a briefing of all United States citizens in the Punjab. At 5:30 P.M., we and our guests drove to the assemblage of citizens at the Roosevelt House, next to the Embassy. Chester Bowles was already speaking when we joined the crowd. He was giving calm reassurances that, in case of emergency and danger, all would be taken care of. And he was asking all of us to go about our business as usual and to make an effort not to contribute in our conversations to the emotional strain of the local Indian citizens.

Carroll and I wrote reassuring letters to our parents but, as he said, "There is not too much point in long and detailed correspondence for a few days, since what we write may not be delivered until it is quite stale." Instead, I sat down at my desk on Thursday midmorning (9 September 1965) and began to write the beginning of an account of activities that were not covered in my letters. Tuesday night gave us some cause for alarm that robbed us of much sleep. Air-raid sirens told us something was amiss, but we remained in our beds. We were told the next morning that a Pakistani plane had been shot down over Delhi.

It is strange how life goes on as usual in the daylight hours, in spite of moments of excitement and apprehension during the nights. Yesterday (still Wednesday) Howard and Al made their scheduled bus ride to Agra and the Taj Mahal, returning at 9:00 P.M. They were told that this would be the last such tour for the present.

Upon their return, they found us on the roof. In comfortable wicker chairs, we continued to enjoy the full moonlight and cool breezes. We had made our arrangements for quick cover in relatively safe spots in our bedroom—Carroll and I under the large table being stored for Jack Sutters, David behind our four neatly covered footlockers. We had also prepared Howard's and Al's palangs so that they could be up-ended against the dining-room table.

We enjoyed visiting for an hour or two. Howard and

Al each related his experiences in Kenya and Tanzania, respectively. Since we had lost sleep the previous night, we retired around 10 or 10:30 and had a good night's sleep until shortly after 4:00 A.M. Then came the wail of the sirens, and in a few moments we had changed our positions to less comfortable but safer ones. The sirens came from different parts of Delhi, including the Safjardang airport a block from our apartment.

This morning we learned that Howard and Al had decided to remain in bed throughout the alert, which lasted about forty minutes before the all-clear signal. Since we heard no bombing, we suspected (all but David) a drill rather than an alert. (Delhi has acquired new sirens, perhaps needing testing.) David went up on the roof afterwards and saw an interesting flare-up in the distance north of Delhi. Early morning news from All India Radio and in the paper threw no light on the alert.

And now I am back to my observation concerning the normal atmosphere of daylight hours. Carroll has gone to the Centre. In front of our house, road workers, consisting of entire families, are moving equipment from completed areas to somewhere further on. While little girls lead or carry toddlers and infants, and mothers carry empty baskets and various tools, men and boys are kicking empty oil drums ahead of them while carrying one on their head. Sometimes, a drum is filled and heavy. This is a noisy procedure but offers entertainment to the workers.

The doorbell just rang and Raghubir admitted our grocery boy. The *dhobi* is rinsing clothes in the bathtub. (We have to gather our tub full of water every morning before noon because the city turns off the water between that time and 4:00 P.M. in some parts of New Delhi.) Howard and Al are touring Delhi and trying to move their flight up from Saturday at 5:30 A.M. to as soon as possible. Most international flights are cancelled or curtailed. David is reading, as I have been doing, and we are hoping that U Thant's presence will help the situation. We are feeling sympathy for our loved ones back home, who may be imagining much worse things than we are experiencing. I am listening to a nice musical program after trying in vain to get news. Shortwave is picking up either entertainment or airplane calls, which I don't like to hear. So I shall return to my paperback.

It took Howard and Al almost a week to get a plane out. They left early one morning for a scheduled flight but had to return shortly before midnight without having found a seat on a plane. Finally, they managed to get away. A card received a week later had been mailed from Bangkok and removed any concern that we had for their safe departure.

Meanwhile, Arjan Das, the Indian secretary at the Quaker House, had arranged for us to attend an absorbing orientation course introducing the culture of India. The AFSC had for several years managed to have their new staff in Delhi invited to the series of lectures, demonstrations, recitals and side-trips arranged for visiting diplomats with their families.

On the first day of orientation, a woman appearing to be in her fifties sat by me and introduced herself as the wife of a man who held a minor post in the German embassy. When she learned that my husband was with the Quaker CONSEM Program in South and Southeast Asia, her face lit up and she exclaimed, "Oh, I am acquainted with the Quakers. Indeed, most Germans have a great appreciation for you people because of your war relief programs—especially the feeding of the children. Yours is a religion with wonderful practices."

I smiled and responded that my husband and I were both Quakers by convincement. I went on to tell how the Friends had given us the emotional and financial support we needed as conscientious objectors to the war. It was almost time for the speaker to be introduced, but the woman had time to whisper, "Sometime, I'd like to hear more about your right to object conscientiously without imprisonment or execution. We had our objectors to the Nazis, too, but they were labeled either traitors or martyrs, depending on one's view of patriotism. And we never found till after the war how many of us there were. If we could only have banded together!"

The conversation had to end there. We never again came together in the large group of attenders at the orientation program. I would have liked to tell her about my year in Munich.

David and I participated in the entire program, including a trip to Agra and the Taj Mahal. Carroll's participation was cut short when he had to leave for an extended trip in preparation for the seminar to be held in Ceylon in December. This meant a long separation and left

David and me on our own in Delhi. That is not entirely correct. By this time, two persons had entered the picture who, in addition to the Ashbys, were to prove very supportive: John Sutters had joined the CONSEM program as bookkeeper and trouble-shooter. Jack, as we soon learned to call him, was an intelligent and perceptive young man, mature enough for me to depend on for advice and assistance and young enough for David to look to for understanding and support. Carroll, too, had found him to be very congenial, and the four of us had quickly become good friends.

Nette Bossert, a woman from Holland and somewhat younger than I, had been serving in India under the Friends Service Council of London as a consultant to the University of Delhi and a lecturer in comparative religion and philosophy. She and I found that we had many common interests and I was always happy when circumstances brought us together. Carroll and Nette shared a similar sense of humor and he enjoyed her company as much as I did.

David's school work and explorations of the city with young friends kept him busy. He still had bouts with homesickness and longing for his girl friend back in the States, but letters were a comfort and he made new friends easily. I had added a private project to my homemaking responsibilities. I had received permission to use the format of a direct language-learning program, *Say It Correctly in* [German]," and hoped to learn enough colloquial Hindi to translate the program into Hindi. That was my main reason for taking lessons in Hindi. This was permanently interrupted, however, by a great misfortune that was to mar our adventure in South and Southeast Asia.

12
GROWTH . . . THROUGH SUFFERING AND NOT DESPAIR
1966

It was years later when I first understood that this phrase, quoted from a speech by Radhakrishnan, was to be the best description of our experience in Southeast Asia. Over three weeks had elapsed since Carroll's departure, on October 3, for Bangkok, Vientiane, Hongkong, Manila (with side-trips elsewhere in the Philippines) and Saigon. I was beginning to get anxious because I had received no word from him. When, finally, three letters arrived at once, I discovered that he had not heard from me, either. We had misunderstood the forwarding instructions. With raised spirits, I was starting another letter when a cable arrived from Carroll in Saigon. He had become ill, probably in Laos, definitely by the Philippines, and was having to return to Delhi three weeks earlier than scheduled.

Weeks of suffering followed. Carroll received expert medical care from Dr. Chako, a physician trained especially to treat tropical diseases. She was a United States citizen, a devout Christian, and the wife of an Indian lawyer. Both Carroll and I had confidence in her. Carroll was trying to go about his daily tasks as the *amoebiasis hystalitica*, which she had diagnosed immediately, was gradually being controlled and, they hoped, eradicated. But David and I, as well as Carroll's friends and colleagues, could see a radical change in him. All enthusiasm and self-confidence seemed to have disappeared, no matter how bravely he tried to hold on to his sense of humor and to put on a cheerful front. My spirits fell daily as I watched him from the balcony, dragging his feet down the walk toward the office, and saw him return, with a dejected air, for lunch. I could not always persuade him to return to the office in the afternoon. Still, I could not accept his growing conviction that he was not up to the job he had come to India to do. I urged him to get out of bed in the morning and to get up from naps during the day. Eventually, David scolded me: "Why don't you get off Dad's back? He's doing the best he can. Can't you see that?"

I awakened to the fact that I might be doing the wrong thing by encouraging Carroll beyond what he considered his capacity. Yet I could not refrain from urging him to continue the work for which I felt him so capable. I could not accept his negative self-assessment and kept on pointing out what he had already accomplished. He had, for one thing, straightened out a personnel problem that had troubled Arjan Das for a long time and had recently received a letter from the London office expressing appreciation for this. I reminded him of this fact but my words did not help. Carroll seemed to be even more dejected and insisted that he could see nothing to do but write a letter of resignation.

All the buoyancy of spirit that I had felt about our Southeast Asian venture had turned into heaviness of heart. Nights were especially difficult, when I lay down on my palang placed as close alongside Carroll's as I could put it and attempted to reach out to him, and was rejected. I had always looked forward to the opportunity for private talks and intimate expressions of feeling without the interruption of daytime duties and other personal relationships. Now, this had changed. Circumstances were driving a wedge between us that I did not know how to remove. Carroll continued to reject my affectionate overtures, sadly but firmly.

Instead of looking to me for encouragement, Carroll grew increasingly impatient with me. I was desolate. Only my attempts to turn inward for spiritual support kept me from collapsing altogether. During the day, I was able to present my customarily optimistic self while Carroll followed Dr. Chako's prescriptions faithfully, going to the office daily, and doing his work as best he could. He put off writing the letter.

When the time came for the CONSEM staff with their families and the directors of Quaker House to leave for the University of Ceylon at Peradeniya, Carroll tried to share in the enthusiasm that the others were feeling. The trip itself was exciting. We took the train to Madras, sharing a three-tiered sleeping car with many Muslim pilgrims as far as Bopal, where they would change to a train bound for Mecca. We flew from Madras to Colombo and then continued by train into the mountains, to Peradenija, a picturesque old city not far from the university.

The subject of the seminar, "Young People in Young Nations," was of general interest to everyone. Those who had seen the movie, *The Bridge on the River Kwai*, looked forward to enjoying the landscape around Colombo and Peradeniya, where it had been filmed. Most of the participants came from India, but many were students from other countries such as Ireland, Denmark, Nepal, Kenya, Israel and even Vietnam. This was the first time that the government of India allowed young women students to participate in a seminar outside their country along with the men. David and I enjoyed watching the young people of Ceylon, who were more westernized than the participants from India, teach the young Indian women the latest popular dances.

The seminar was housed in a beautiful building constructed around three sides of a quadrangle with a lovely pool and gardens. It was connected with other buildings by arcades that went completely around every building so that, rain or shine, we could spend all free time outdoors if we wished. A small group of participants held early morning meetings for worship under an arcade facing mountains colored by the sunrise. I have never forgotten the spirit of these gatherings, which renewed my own spirit daily.

New Year's Day proved to be an especially historic time. By then, we were back in Colombo to spend a couple of days at the YWCA. We were fortunate enough to witness the celebration of the change to the old Buddhist calendar and the resumption of the Buddhist name Sri Lanka, by which the island has been known since.

Running parallel to these thrilling experiences was, for me, the terrible, private experience with Carroll. In his work, he played a role. I was astonished at the positive contribution he was able to make, especially on the night set aside for answering the inevitable question at conferences and seminars: Who are the Quakers? Who are the people responsible for this program? His remarks were simple and brief, but I felt they were the most appropriate and clear of all made on the subject that evening. In private, the role was dropped. Always, he felt that he was a failure. No matter how I might express, in private, my pride in his successes and my denial of his "failures," he could respond only with an inflexible spirit of despair and a growing air of impatience, almost anger, toward my positive attitude.

The climax came when I became aware of the irrational anxieties he was expressing about our approaching departure for India. We were on the train taking us down from the mountains to Colombo. The scenery was breathtaking and I suddenly exclaimed: "David . . . Carroll . . . look!" In a nearby stream, elephants were bathing. David responded with enthusiasm. Carroll hardly looked up. He spoke in a low, but excited, tone of voice: "Mary, I'm worried. We may never get away from here. If we can just make it through customs without getting arrested . . . Are you sure you and David haven't bought anything more? You promised . . . nothing 'til we get back to Delhi." (He had been disturbed when David and Ann had bought some unset semiprecious stones, as inexpensive as they were beautiful—the usual tourist purchase.) I assured him that I had bought only an inexpensive cotton bag, my only souvenir of Kandy and of the entire seminar.

Throughout the New Year's celebration, his mind could not be diverted from his fear of the return trip. Because our sleeping quarters at the YWCA were on a screened porch, he was more distressed than delighted by the fireworks that David admired. Carroll felt they were a threat to our safety. The rockets were so close that even I shared his alarm a little, but not to the extent of his anxiety that ever more dominated his mood. At last, completely discouraged, I decided to write a long letter to Nora Booth, the staff person to whom Carroll sent his reports. I knew that Warren had already written three letters expressing his concern about Carroll. It was time, I believed, to admit my own feelings of alarm. Carroll wrote a short note saying that he would write a longer letter of explanation later, after we had returned from Ceylon/Sri Lanka.

Some relief came to Carroll after this. On Friday, February 11, the two of us flew to Lucknow. Upon the advice of the staff psychiatrist in Philadelphia, we visited Nur Manzil Clinic to consult a doctor recommended by Dr. Chako. The clinic was a busy place. Still, the doctor was able to keep a brief morning appointment. Although we had much to communicate in a brief period, we felt that our interview with the psychiatrist was very important. We both came away feeling that he might be better able to help than anyone else at the moment. It was decided that after a week Carroll would return alone for a short stay, and then, later, I would probably return, too, since the doctor liked to work with both husband and wife in a case involving either spouse.

The trip to Lucknow and Nur Manzil took place over the weekend of February 11-13. According to my journal, I was busy writing letters the following week, not only to family members, but also to Guilford faculty and students. Writing letters was difficult at this time because I did not want to worry family and friends about Carroll's condition. One letter, addressed but never sent, was to Laurama, on the CONSEM staff at the home office. The entire letter is too long to give in full; however, what is here is quoted verbatim:

15 February 1966

Dear Laurama,

I would give a great deal, Laurama, if we could only have a face-to-face talk with those of you who meant so much to us during our orientation. I, especially, feel at present that I can never write as freely as I expressed myself to you when Carroll and I were there and were facing the future in India with equal enthusiasm. I do not know whether or what to write. I find my role as wife a difficult one in this particular situation. I desire only to assure Carroll of my firm faith in his capabilities for this Program. To encourage one's husband to complete what he has set out to do seems the proper thing for me to do. It's in line with what I personally want, also. In spite of all this, I realize that I cannot and should not impose my will on his. I hope that we can both wait for the revelation of the divine Will we should be serving in our respective ways, if we can just get our respective wills in tune with God's!

At this point, I'll close. I cannot sensibly plan any further. I am seeking patience and (but?) I am so far an incurable optimist.

Sincerely,
Mary

By February 21, a letter to Ed Burrows showed more resignation:

. . . It's hard for me to believe that we'd be sent or allowed by Providence to come so far and at the expense of the AFSC just for our own instruction in living. . . . We are both in a quandary. But I have learned one thing: that

even those who are united in marriage must sometimes
leave each other the privacy of soul to make independent
decisions. This is the particular lesson that I had to learn
in respect to Carroll.

I kept hoping that Carroll would recover soon, so I wrote about
sounds, sights and aromas of India. The roof never ceased to be my
favorite observation post. I spent hours there alone. While Carroll
was away, I awakened early and climbed the polished granite stairs
daily to seek a few degrees of coolness in the gray dawn. Across the
broad street lay the Karbala, a grassy field enclosed by a low brick
wall. The Karbala served many Muslims as a sacred place for an annual ceremony where they burned and buried replicas of the tomb of
Hussein, Mohammed's grandson. A Muslim tailor, whom Helen had
sent to me with high recommendations for any kind of personal sewing, had tried to explain its significance, but, according to my own
observation, it served also regularly as a "privy en plein air" for
dhobi-clad squatters who felt well hidden in the tall grass behind the
wall.

Solitude gave me the opportunity for the contemplative moments I had treasured since childhood. My mind dwelt on the varieties of religion represented by the people around me, on the varieties
of dress and skin color. How striking it was to see the fair-skinned,
blue-eyed Nette Bossert from Holland, dressed in the sari to which
she had grown accustomed, alongside the many shades of bronze,
brown, and black natives in saris, punjabis, dhotis, or Western dress.

I soon discovered that all religious holidays seemed to be observed or tolerated by everyone. Holi, which was celebrated in
March, impressed me especially because it resembled a concentrated
Fasching in one respect: any and all class distinctions seemed to fall
away on that day. Everyone, down to the lowest caste, was free to
celebrate this Hindu holiday by spraying colors in liquid or powder
form on anyone else who ventured into the streets. Warren had
warned us to stay indoors or wear old clothes; he had had a white suit
sprayed with rainbow hues shot from syringes and air-hoses.

Raghubir, of course, had the day off, as everyone was expected
to have. However, during the day, he abruptly appeared in the apartment, where I was sitting absorbed in a book. He approached me
with a broad smile on his brown face saying, "You should have the
chance to celebrate Holi with us. Here . . . " and he leaned over me as

he extended an arm toward me. He had red powder cupped in his left hand, into which he had dipped his right forefinger. "Here . . . look at me." Gently he pressed his finger onto the center of my forehead. "Now, please look into the mirror."

Feeling strangely moved, I stood up and walked to a mirror in the hallway. There, centered just above the brows, was the tilak, a small red dot. Raghubir was gazing at me with serious approval. "Now you are one of us." He smiled again and left as quickly as he had come.

I wore the slightly smudged religious symbol for the rest of the day. By respecting the simple gesture of this young Hindu, I felt that I was sharing concretely in the universal human attempt at religious expression. Then my thoughts turned to another sharing, perhaps at a more mature level, between the Quaker, John Woolman, and Chief Papunchang, a native American Indian. After meeting in silence for worship with some members of his tribe and their visiting Friends, the chief remarked, "I love to feel where words come from." I understood better now this awareness of the Spirit from where all symbols come.

* * *

David coped with his father's illness better than I. Upon turning eighteen, he had received his international driver's license and was driving to St. Stephen's daily. The arrival in Delhi of the Citroën 2CV had boosted his morale more than his parents'. (Arjan Das had phoned many times before discovering that it had been sitting in Bombay for weeks—months?—accruing storage charges!) David also spent spare time with his peers. Just before his dad's return to Nur Manzil, I had invited his favorite classmate, Raj, to lunch. Raj was affable, yet a serious student, and made a favorable impression on both Carroll and me. We were already pleased with Melissa and Ann, his other close companions.

I spent many unhappy hours during the week of Carroll's absence. Raghubir, however, was helpful during his working hours and on one occasion provided me with needed emotional support. Again, it was a simple gesture on his part. I had learned, I believed, to hide my unhappiness from others around me and indulged in tears only when alone. On this day I was feeling despondent after a short interval of welcome distraction by the visit to "my" roof of a solitary sparrow that reminded me of North Carolina. It had perched briefly on the balustrade, looked at me quizzically and then flown away. Two crows in the neem tree closest to the house had been too preoccupied with each other to pay me any attention. So I was feeling sorry for myself and was busy wiping away the tears that would not stop. Suddenly, Raghubir was standing there with a glass of steaming tea, thick with sugar. "Pardon me," he said gently, "but this may help you to be feeling better. It always helps me."

I took the tea and thanked the thoughtful bearer, who left immediately. It was the only time that he ever appeared on the roof during my moments there. He had chosen the right moment now, for I drank the tea and the tears disappeared. With lifted spirits, I picked up a pad and pen lying on a wicker table at my side and completed the poem that I had begun some time ago.

SEPARATION

Together we had flown with the sun westward
(flame-feathered skies from San Francisco
to Honolulu   and one day dropped
like a knitter's stitch before Tokyo)
to this new   this ancient   this timeless India.

From the day of the letter   poetic dreams
of heroic dedication had inspired
prosaic preparations:
leaves of absence from pedagogical duties
to be exchanged for leaves of the neem tree
for sheesham and sandalwood
project-briefings inspired and practical
study of bold outlines for months ahead
shots   to thwart all things preventable
(but none for culture-shock or elusive amoebae
no provision for the uninvited guest
Entamoeba Hystalitica).

So yesterday brought us goodbyes
choking on dust as it swallowed the plane
returning him alone to Nur Manzil
oasis for desiccated psyches
thirsting for familiar fountains.

On the day of Carroll's return from Lucknow, Mike Yarrow arrived from the Philadelphia office. His visit was wonderful therapy for us. He spent the time needed for objective, yet caring, counsel—

valuable because of his years of experience relating to problems like depression. He also took time to arrange a trip to Agra so that Carroll could visit the Taj Mahal, which he had missed seeing, and all three of us could visit Fatehpur-Sikri, "which all should see before dying." By the time of his departure, two things were clear: Carroll had been restored almost to his old feelings of confidence; I was content that, in May, we would participate in the Conference for Diplomats in Kathmandu, and that soon after we would return to Guilford College.

The months remaining in India were happier, though still frustrating. I never mailed some of my letters, like the one to Laurama. I did not want to cause undue worry for those who were far from the scene. Jack, Nette and the Ashbys, as well as the Millers at Quaker House, continued to offer the support of their friendship. Jack, especially, became very close to all three of us. We were almost as disappointed as he was when the decision was made for him to remain in the office while the rest of the staff, with their families, took part in the Conference for Diplomats in Kathmandu.

Because of its pioneer aspect, the conference made headlines in the local paper. This type of Quaker conference, however, was not new. Conferences for diplomats had been held for many years in Washington, D.C. The idea is to bring together diplomats representing a variety of nations, without any of the news media present. A subject of general interest is chosen (in Kathmandu it concerned problems of developing nations), leaders and consultants with expertise on the topic are invited, and opportunities are given for free and informal discussion, for recreation, and for sightseeing. At this conference, the participants had the privilege of meeting Willi Unsold and hearing him tell of his climbing Mount Everest. He also showed slides of the thrilling event.

Everyone was excited to be in the Himalayas and to take a trip to a spot within sight of Mount Everest. But the main function of the gathering was to allow diplomats to get to know one another as persons, to approach problems from different perspectives, and to have friendly arguments without fear of being misquoted in the public press. In this way, many long-held prejudices were surmounted. Best of all, for me, was to see Carroll's growing enthusiasm and return to better health.

For us, the Conference for Diplomats was an idyllic period of ten days in May sandwiched between intervals of concentrated frustrations met in connection with our early departure from India. It took us five days, waiting several hours on each, to pay income tax in advance. After getting permission elsewhere, we went to the Bank of India to pay. Carroll came out from there with a temporary receipt for the payment he had give them. This "chit" had to be exchanged for a valid receipt, on the fifth and final day!

* * *

Saying goodbye to Arjan Das was like saying goodbye to India personified. I had become fond of this "Quindu" ("Hindu/Quaker") as some lovingly called him. He was the office manager of Quaker House serving both British and American Friends. It was he who made most of the behind-the-scenes arrangements for local meetings, for travel to meetings elsewhere in India and, sometimes, out of the country, and for business transactions where a translator was needed. In any case, he was always there to counsel those who needed and sought advice in dealings with Indians. He managed the household servants and was at his desk to receive visitors. He was the one who welcomed new directors and bade them farewell, remaining the only continuous "spirit of Quaker House."

Although he admired the Quakers and understood (indeed, often exemplified) their Christian faith and practice very well, he never could leave his Hindu religion. Nor did he need to. I came to see that there was something about the Hindu faith so comprehensive as to be able to assimilate other religions without causing them to lose their identity, with only exclusiveness seeming to vanish. For the Hindu, the Divine One is speaking as Krishna: "When goodness grows weak, when evil increases, I make myself a body. In every age I may return to deliver the body, to destroy the sin of the sinner, to establish the righteous."

Many Quakers besides me may accept this as a description of the constant accessibility of the Light for those who seek its grace. It appears as the Comforter, as Jesus promised, the Inner Companion, the Mystic Confidant (as North Carolina Quaker Algie Newlin called it) or, as George Fox wrote in his Journal, the Inner Teacher. "When my goodness grows weak," I can say to myself, "when evil threatens to overcome me, the 'Divine One' is present to support me."

We said our goodbyes on June 3, 1966. David was eager to get home so flew all the way—the only one of us to fly around the globe. Carroll and I stayed in London briefly before taking the *Statendam*.

SOMETHING TANGIBLE

What am I doing with this lovely screen
from India?
Ashoka's lions, central in the scene
but minus the pillar calling for peace,
delicate carvings out of sheeshamwood,
other exotic animals, in pairs, which could
remind us of Noah—
how many children's hands
cut out these peacocks and these elephants,
these haughty camels of the desert sands?
(and how can camels
fitting cramped dimensions
for the carvers from the Rajasthan
still look so condescending?)
How is it that this lacy screen
should now be lending
its beauty to a Quaker home?
How has it come
to bring chinar-leaves
to the Carolinas?

Perhaps it's easier to share
a tangible creation
with a friend's admiring stare,
to let the wonders of a strange land
breathe through the ornaments
under a caressing hand,
to let a poke of the finger
through a leafy vine
evoke the charm of India
caught in this frame.

If only I had left behind
something of the same,
something to remind
India
of me
and of my love for her.

13

UPS AND DOWNS

1967–1982

After India, there was a series of ups and downs. Carroll returned to teaching and was enjoying it with a new appreciation enhanced by good health. At the same time, Quakers in the area were looking forward to an event that would draw the broader Greensboro community. The Friends World Committee for Consultation had scheduled its Fourth World Conference for 1967, to which over eight hundred delegates would be traveling to meet on the Guilford College campus. In addition, several hundred visiting Friends would meet on the campus of the University of North Carolina in Greensboro. Carroll was involved in planning various musical programs and I was on Eva Newlin's committee to make arrangements for delegates to visit in homes throughout the monthly meetings of North Carolina.

When the time came for this exciting gathering of Friends, I found myself for most of the occasion in a planning room in Founders Hall. There I made sure that single people did not get placed in double beds and married couples did not get separated for the weekend of visitation. Another problem arose, but rather rarely: there were a few who specified some reluctance to entertain folk of a different color. Since there were plenty of fair-skinned Friends to go around, this reluctance was obligingly, but sorrowfully, kept in mind.

Although I missed most of the daytime programs, I did get to participate in one thrilling occasion. Carroll and I had been attending a weekly silent vigil with a group of citizens protesting the war in

Vietnam. Our group of around fifteen or twenty men, women and, sometimes, children represented no one religious or political group, although the AFSC regional office did provide much of the literature handed to passersby willing to receive it. During the conference we were joined by more than a hundred international attenders, so that the line stretched from the front of the court house around three sides of the city block. We felt deeply moved to be numbered among such a wide variety of persons joining in this public demonstration for peace.

Carroll made a special contribution to the conference when United Nations General Secretary U Thant gave a public address at the Greensboro Coliseum, the only public building large enough to accommodate the expected crowd. Carroll had been asked to play the organ and had carefully chosen the music he would play while U Thant was present. Before the arrival of the General Secretary, he used some majestic hymns appropriate for Quakers but not especially for non-Christians. For U Thant's entrance and departure, he played his adaptation of the closing peaceful passage from Malcolm Arnold's "The United Nations" as recorded for Gerard Hoffnung's Interplanetary Music Festival (1958). I was not the only one deeply affected by this. At the conclusion of the prelude, there was a long moment of silence preparing the mood for the speech to follow.

One other aspect of this world gathering that had special meaning for both the Ashbys and us was seeing again many of the friends we had made in South and Southeast Asia. Tayeko Yamanouchi and Nette Bossert were both there. Then, to our pleasant surprise, Nette was asked to stay on as Lecturer in Comparative Religion for the fall semester at Guilford. Before returning to India and after some traveling on her own, she joined us in travel through New England.

* * *

Carroll's health, fortunately, was excellent for all of this. Then, early in 1968 he had the first symptoms of a recurrence of amoebic problems. A local doctor prescribed the same medication that had been effective in India. It worked successfully for a while. However, when Carroll felt that the symptoms were returning again, this doctor doubted that the original amoeba was present. So Carroll went to a parasitologist in Chapel Hill, who identified the same amoeba *hystalitica*. A new drug was added in combination with the one originally prescribed. The two drugs threw Carroll into a psychotic state.

It could have been a permanent disaster, according to an article sent to us by the parasitologist. Carroll was one of over fifty cases of this reaction to that combination of chemicals. A few had remained permanently psychotic. To our relief, his recovery was rapid—within three days, surprisingly—and we could look back on the episode with a certain amount of grim humor whenever I described some of his bizarre behavior. I had found him once lecturing, with all seriousness and in erudite philosophical terms, into a wastebasket, which he was holding, slightly tipped, before his face. This happened at the time of the assassination of Martin Luther King, and Carroll was certain that King had escaped his assailant and was hiding in a closet in the hospital! (The survival of King, would, of course, have been Carroll's fervent wish.) For both of us, it was easy to laugh, afterwards, when I told him less significant details, such as his pouring buttermilk into his coffee and drinking it with relish.

Carroll has never again had to go through this kind of psychotic episode—so suddenly come and gone, and brought on solely by the administration of dangerous medication. Since India, the two of us have experienced Carroll's monopolar cycle of short clinical depressions and, since 1979, a bipolar cycle including euphoric upswings, with periods of well balanced and productive behavior that last about two years. For me, this has meant corresponding changes in my own personality. Looking back over our married life, we recognize that our time in India was its critical point; we catalog everything in our marriage as Before India (B.I.) or After India (A.I.).

During a halcyon period (A.I.), we enjoyed two delightful trips abroad. One, in 1970, was with Jack Sutters. In London, we rented a Mini, as in 1963 (B.I.). We drove from England through Wales, ferried to Ireland, and drove clockwise around the coast from Dublin to Larne. Ferrying to Scotland, we had a memorable reunion in Edinburgh with Margaret Gibbins, whom we had met at the Friends World Conference.

In Wales, I had been touched with gratitude when Carroll offered to drive a little out of the way to visit the home of my Munich friend, Dyfri Rees. With the help of a charming old lady across the street, I was able to learn that Dyfri was happily married and had moved to Oxford with his family. Since his parents had died, he no longer visited his native home, but I left a message about my visit with the neighbor, just in case! I no longer had to entertain the sad thought that he might have been killed in the war or that I might have broken his heart when I wrote him about Carroll so many years ago.

The other trip lasted the entire summer of 1971 and took us, by Eurail Pass and plane, all over Europe and to the Soviet Union. We traveled with Polly and Whitfield Cobb, their sixteen-year-old daughter, and her girl friend of the same age. After we all had chosen the places we wanted to visit, Polly and I spent months writing letters to hotels and pensions. Only one date was fixed at the beginning: we had to be in Vienna at the time of the performance of the Lippizaner horses. Whit had tickets for everyone.

Carroll and I were happy to revisit some of our favorite places with our friends, and Polly's interest and fluency in Russian enriched our visits to Leningrad and Moscow. One incident concerning Polly's enthusiasm for spreading goodwill personally among the Russian people was a source of amusement and a reason for rejoicing, too. She had brought peace propaganda, which, incidentally, had slowed our entry through customs, and was intending to distribute it quietly. Much to everyone's surprise, as we entered the lobby of our first hotel, we saw on a bulletin board the familiar logo and slogan of "Another Mother for Peace," which made up a good part of Polly's propaganda. Some other mother or father had apparently preceded Polly with the logo, already on its way to becoming global.

A detailed account of events of the summer could itself fill a book. I kept a journal in installments, which I mailed as letters to Mother. Two vignettes from among our private adventures appeared later in a journal for Russian studies edited by Polly. One tells of our being driven at a mad pace to the theater in Leningrad, the sole passengers in a tourist bus whose driver had witnessed our frantic and futile efforts to hail a taxi at our hotel. The compassionate rescuer also refused to accept any fare or tip for his service. The other tells of Carroll's being invited to play the organ prelude for the overflowing congregation of Moscow's largest Protestant church—just because I had remarked to the English-speaking hostess that my husband was a church organist. How could that kind woman have known that Carroll really was a good organist and would perform well?

There is one more vignette, not of Russia, but a test of the Cobb-Feagins friendship and the narrow passing of that test. Carroll and I held the vouchers for boat passage from Bari to Dubrovnik. The four of us had agreed upon this arrangement because Polly and Whit, after a stay in Rome, would be arriving with the girls in Bari later than we would. We would be coming from Palermo and could exchange the vouchers for our tickets before the arrival of our friends. In this way, our party of six would be ready to depart on that same evening, Friday.

Carroll and I had divided our time in Sicily between Siracusa and Palermo. Reconstructing later what had happened, we remembered having missed a city tour of Palermo on our first morning and having been told that we could take the same tour the following morning. This we had verified by a quick glance at our letter of reservation for the hotel there. We had taken the tour and spent a lovely afternoon at the beach within sight of Mount Rosalie. Then we had taken a night-train around the instep of Italy.

As Carroll was reading his Cook's *Continental Timetable* on the train the next morning, he suddenly looked at me with a horrified expression on his face and exclaimed: "This has to be Friday, or something is radically wrong!" I insisted it was Saturday until I realized, almost immediately, that we had misread our time schedule in Palermo. We had failed to pick up the tickets on Friday. Were Polly, Whit, and the girls still waiting in Bari? Or had they managed to get tickets and to catch the boat on time? Throughout the rest of the train ride, Carroll and I were anxiously awaiting the answer. When we arrived, I was not sure whether I wanted to see our friends waiting for us or preferred to find them already gone from Bari.

They were gone. But they had left a definite impression behind them. Upon inquiry, we learned of our friends' panic at the railroad station and later, of Polly's indignant remonstrations at the maritime office (where there was a record of their reservations). They had to purchase more tickets and had departed in a flurry. We discovered, also, that there were no more crossings, even by plane, until Monday. So we sent a telegram to the Cobbs and had an unexpected weekend in Bari with an unanticipated opportunity to visit the tomb of Saint Nicholas.

When we arrived in Dubrovnik, Whit and Polly were there to greet us. They gravely handed us our telegram. It was addressed to Colonel Whitfield and announced "Arriving at 4.00 P.M. on Tintoretto with incrediboble story!" The "incrediboble" message served to leaven the misadventure with our laughter. Besides, the Cobbs had found their accommodations in Dubrovnik (arranged by me) so delightful and had spent such an enjoyable weekend that all was already forgiven. The Cobbs were relieved to learn that we had not been in an accident.

Weeks later, I succeeded in getting refunds for the Cobb tickets. I felt we did not deserve any. Whit surprised us, however, at Christmas, with refunds for us, too.

* * *

In the fall of 1972, after North Carolina Friends Yearly Meeting, Carroll took an overdose of a tranquilizer. If he had not left a note, discovered later, we could not have known that he himself had caused the deep seventy-two hour coma. He did not remember writing it.

"You know," he said sadly, "all I can remember is being desperate for a good night's sleep. . . . I couldn't go on without that. Life is impossible without sleep."

From that time on, Carroll was resigned to the probability of cycles of depression. I reminded him of Uncle Mort's dire prediction. Whether those "damned eggs" were responsible or not, doctors agreed that all safe—and one not so safe—means had been used to eradicate the parasites and the need now was to concentrate on controlling the mood swings with lithium. Early in 1974, when Carroll felt again all the symptoms of a coming depression, he voluntarily entered a hospital, where he could be prevented from repeating his attempt at a self-cure. He was given a leave from teaching, which, hindsight revealed, was actually extended beyond the necessary time. But everyone wanted to be sure that the cycle was broken. Lithium seemed to be effective and its side effects controllable.

* * *

Meanwhile, since India, both Carroll, Jr. and David had married, and both had married daughters of college faculty. Carroll, Jr. and Louise Hilty had known each other since childhood. And he said when he came to tell us the really surprising news, "It's almost like marrying the girl next door . . . only she lives over the hill at the end of the road. We just fell in love with each other."

I could hardly keep from reminding him of the vain struggle the Hiltys and we had gone through when we tried to get our children to play with each other while they were young. Now, here was our older son announcing his plan to marry a Hilty daughter. And, as he said, "Louise is more than pretty, you know. She is really a very good girl. There aren't many like her these days."

He added a few extra days to the Fourth of July holidays allowed from his job at Simpson Printers. Louise gave notice to the law firm where she worked as a filing clerk. They were married in New Garden Meeting House, with her father, a recorded minister, performing the ceremony. The wedding reminded me of my own. It was sweetly solemn and attended primarily by close friends and relatives. Fair weather favored their week at Myrtle Beach, South Carolina, to which they often would return in later years. Their daughter arrived promptly ten months after their honeymoon and brought much happiness to her grandparents on both sides.

David and Tanya had become good friends at Guilford when they were students. Her name came to her from her mother, a Russian by birth. Her mother had been captured and was employed as a nurse by US Army forces in Vienna, where Richard Ward met her. The tall, striking woman attracted the attention of the even taller, handsome young soldier; they were married and he brought her to the States.

Tanya was an unusually mature student as well as an alluring and talented young woman. David was working at Sears to defray dormitory expenses and quickly figured out that he could afford an inexpensive student apartment just as easily. With Tanya's cooking and sewing skills, they could live more cheaply together than apart. And so they convinced their parents that it would be a good thing for them to marry and complete their college days together. They, too, were married at New Garden. Of their own accord, they had a traditional Quaker wedding, for which Tanya made not only her own gown but also those of her attendants, her best friend and her two sisters. I was more pleased, probably, than they would ever know to see the bridal pair rise at their chosen time and say their vows quietly but distinctly. It was something I had never dreamed of witnessing.

Mother, I believe, felt especially blessed to be present. A great-grandmother now and a beloved member of the community, she presented a lovely picture during the reception, as she presided at the punch bowl and greeted relatives and friends of the campus and the meeting. I exchanged happy smiles with her and hoped that she shared the extent of my joy in the occasion. It seemed only yesterday that I had longed for a daughter. Now I had two wonderful daughters-in-law and an adorable two-year-old granddaughter named Debora Ann.

A close bond developed between Mother and little Debbie. Her parents, nevertheless, managed to keep her from being spoiled either by her great-grandmother or by the two sets of grandparents—all in close proximity. Mother had always known how to communicate with children. She had been baby-sitter for neighborhood parents in College Park and had become the favorite aunt of a multitude of nieces and nephews, great nieces and great nephews. Wherever she went, she was discovered by children to be one of their own kind, someone to play with and to share secrets with.

In retrospect, I have always been glad that Carroll, Jr. and Louise never begrudged the time Debbie spent with her great-grandmother Brown. It turned out that the child had only five years in which to enjoy this privilege. Mother lived those remaining years fully, rich in friends and fortunate in continued vivacity. Her only health problem concerned digestion. Most of the time, she felt well enough to take her daily walk through the campus or by Granddaddy's old path through the woods to the shopping area. And she was one of the few persons who used the infrequent bus to Greensboro. She preferred to be as independent as her health and advanced age permitted.

In late September of 1973, she had one of her attacks of "stomach trouble." She consented to being driven to the hospital. "I might as well take advantage of Medicare for once! I don't want you to keep on having to fix my food in a blender," she said to me. "And I'm getting pretty sick of oatmeal."

After one week in the hospital, she was ready to come home to her apartment. On Sunday, October 7, a week after her return home, Carroll and I experienced the first tragedy among our circle of close friends: our neighbors, Cora Worth and David Parsons, were killed instantly in an unavoidable automobile accident. Cora Worth had visited Mother on that very afternoon and had promised to return, with David, for a visit with Carroll and me in the evening. I did not know how to share this sad news with Mother. Cora Worth's mother had died in August—the last of Mother's campus friends to be lost to her in a series of recent deaths. How could she bear the shock of these two untimely deaths? So I waited until Thursday to explain the steady stream of persons walking past her window to the front door of the house. They were coming to pay their respects to Cora Worth's and David's college-age daughter. She was staying with us until her brother could be reached in Algiers, where he and his bride were serving with the AFSC. It seemed more inconsiderate to let Mother wonder why I was having so many callers during her illness than to tell her what had happened. She accepted the news calmly and expressed her appreciation for my wish to spare her news of the sorrow as long as I could. There was a hint of disbelief in her voice as she spoke, and she never brought up the subject after she was told about the two memorial services, at the college and at New Garden.

On Saturday evening of that same week, Carroll and I were invited to a campus affair. Throughout most of that afternoon, Mother had lain on her lawn chair in the sun. Unknown to me, Carroll had taken a snapshot of her as she lay there, partially covered by her favorite pink stole that we had brought her from Ireland. She presented a picture of tranquility—her beautiful white hair still curling around her face, slightly flushed from the sun, and her reclining figure against a background of green moss and autumn leaves. It was almost as though Carroll knew it would be his last glimpse of her. But when I asked him about it later, he said he did not know what had prompted him to take the picture.

I did not know, either, why I chose, at the last minute, to stay home instead of accompanying Carroll to the campus program. I invited Mother to join me for our favorite TV show, *Mary Tyler Moore*. Both of us fell asleep in our chairs before Carroll returned home. When I walked with her to her apartment, I noticed how fragile she had become. Although we were the same height, she weighed less than 90 pounds as compared to my 120. Mother and daughter roles were reversed as I tucked her into bed and gave her what was to be my last kiss. When I went to her room on Sunday morning, October 14, I found her lying by her bed. She had died quickly and seemingly without much violence during the night as she was leaving her bed. Her death was caused by a heart infarction. When we told Carroll, Jr. the news, he said to me, "Mother, I am not surprised, really. Grandmother said to me last week, 'I know a secret that I am not telling anybody.' Then she looked at me very strangely and sadly. I had a feeling that I knew what she was talking about. I'm sure now."

* * *

In the summer of 1974, while Carroll was still on disability leave from regular teaching, I took on the responsibility of co-directing a summer school in East/West Germany for Guilford and other college or university students. The other director was a young professor from the University of North Carolina in Greensboro. I would not have undertaken this without Carroll's help. During his depression, his psychiatrist (a former student of his) had turned him over to a doctor new to our community. This doctor had managed quickly to assure Carroll that he was definitely going to get well, had him dismissed from the hospital, and persuaded us to take on the new, challenging project. The depression lifted almost simultaneously with our departure. The summer school project was successfully repeated in 1975 and 1976, the last year the young professor was to accompany us. We enlarged the program to include other German-speaking countries and took the students also to Vienna and Bern. By this time, Carroll had resumed teaching his regular courses at the college.

In connection with our recurrent trips to Europe, we continued a practice that we began when we joined the CONSEM Program in South and Southeast Asia (a practice neglected only in 1963). We asked for traveling minutes from New Garden Friends Meeting and North Carolina Yearly Meeting. We had not realized to what extent our attendance at Friends meetings would enrich visits to what became our favorite continental cities: Paris, Munich, Vienna, Dresden, Berlin East and West. It was especially heartwarming to keep close contact with Friends behind the Iron Curtain, who felt isolated. There were around fifty in the entire German Democratic Republic, and when these Friends gathered for their annual meeting in Schwiedeborg, they regularly sent us a postcard with greetings and signatures of all present. By the time of my retirement from teaching, I was corresponding with several of these Friends as well as one in Erfurt. My friend in Erfurt was the only Quaker of that city until her aging father came to live with her, and another in Prague, who was our hostess for our one visit to that city in 1971.

* * *

During our later travels, I missed being able to write my long journal/letters to Mother. Even if she had been alive, the responsibilities of administration and of teaching, counseling, and befriending these groups of summer school students made such letter writing impossible. The responsibilities were enormous, but the rewards were greater. One of the greatest joys was the annual reunion with Aennchen and Walter Kowitz.

Another pleasure came when Claude Shotts, director of Guilford's off-campus programs, introduced us to the German president of Munich's Columbus Society, which offered hospitality to foreign students. Karl Fischer had survived World War II, into which he had been drafted at an early age, without any physical wounds. Now he was carrying out a pledge to foster friendships between his own German students of English and students from the United States. Every summer, while we were in Munich with our students, he would introduce the young visitors to that city's cathedrals, monuments, wine taverns and beer halls, along with the neighboring Alps. His cultural interests were apparent in his enthusiastic presentations of the art and history of the environs. But he had developed since the war a spirit of remorse, almost guilt, expressed in bitter remarks. "I blame myself," he once said, "for not shooting Hitler when I had the chance. As an armed soldier, I could have shot him at the very outset of the war. I was that close to him, more than once!"

His expressions on the subject of Nazism and its insidious influence on the masses of German citizens were of shocking contrast to his expressions of appreciation for German culture in general. I said to him, as soon as I felt sufficiently well acquainted to do so, "Violent language and violent acts don't belong to your character, Karl. I just can't imagine your killing anyone, even Hitler."

Nevertheless, hindsight made it impossible for Karl Fischer to feel anything but regret that he had not done away with Hitler while he had the opportunity. I did not pursue the argument with him. I changed the subject to commend him for continuing to host our students and to foster good relations among the younger generation. I was especially grateful for his taking us all to the rotunda of the university where I had studied years before. Pointing to a modest plaque with a vase holding a single rose, he explained, "This commemorates a brave though futile attempt to overthrow Hitler. A few students and a professor founded the underground movement called the White Rose. They were caught early one morning in this very rotunda dropping leaflets with a call to revolt. As ringleaders, they were speedily executed—beheaded. The circle in front of the university is named for them: die Geschwister Scholl Platz."

I remembered my carefree, yet concerned, Junior Year in Germany, in 1937 and 1938. How sincerely my friends and I had shared our hopes and fears as students in Bavaria! Could we have foreseen *Kristallnacht* only a few months ahead? Or the "holocaust"? I thought not. I had never been the slightest bit clairvoyant, only perceptive and sometimes apprehensive, but always optimistic.

During a visit to Berlin, we met Frau Olga Halle, who was well into her eighties. I learned later that Frau Halle's daughter, Anna Sabine, was writing her own account of what the Berlin Friends Meeting under the leadership of her mother, had done to counteract the influence of Nazism. Anna Sabine Halle had been a part of a group of children who had met regularly in a room at the Quaker Bureau. A few of them were, like herself, children of Quakers; the others were from Jewish families and from families who resisted Hitler. Here they had shared in activities free of Nazi influences on

Hitler youth until the war brought a sad end to their fellowship. I was deeply touched by the story and was happy to be able to translate it for publication in the United States after it had appeared in Germany. It provides evidence that there were more German citizens who were repelled by the inhumane propaganda and acts of the Nazis and who tried to do what they could to repudiate or remedy these evils than could be known at the time.

* * *

Whenever I could find the time, traveling and teaching stimulated me to further writing. In an article for the *Guilford Review*, I described at length a type of "peripatetic pedagogy," as I called it. Venturing abroad with students meant leaving behind the fixed setting of assigned class and office space, and familiar eating and sleeping arrangements. It meant entering into constantly shifting scenarios. Something of the wizardry of an Alexander Calder was required to create a pedagogically pleasing "mobile" with a balance of stability and flexibility.

The itinerant teacher has the opportunity, indeed the need, to teach values. For example, one day, as several of our students were walking across the street from a national monument in East Berlin, they broke into the goose step in mocking imitation of the changing of the guards taking place at the time. We had to point out that it is important to respect the patriotic feelings of others as well as our own. How ironic it was that a Jewish member of the group was not aware of the fact that this monument, with its eternal flame and guard, was erected in memory of those who had been victims of fascism and militarism and was sacred to those who wanted never again to participate in racist and belligerent acts. All that Carroll had to do, however, to bring the group to an awareness of their disrespect was to ask the question, "How would you feel if visiting students from Russia or any other foreign country were to make fun publicly in front of the guard at the tomb of the Unknown Soldier in Arlington?"

In my article, I discussed the opportunity for teacher and students alike to notice a new light thrown onto values such as freedom. We often hear United States citizens say proudly, "It's a free country." Does the word "free" have the same meaning in terms like the Freie Deutsche Jugend, a youth group in East Germany, and the Freie Universitaet in West Germany?—Perhaps, some of us may say, in theory,—but in practice? Or, the value of democracy, which may mean one thing to us and another to the citizens of the Deutsche

Demokratische Republik. "The peripatetic teacher," I concluded, "must always be ready to emulate Socrates by asking the perceptive question and by encouraging the students to do the same, as they moved into changing environments."

* * *

As much as Carroll and I enjoyed our summers in Europe, we suggested that another couple take the German studies group abroad while we used the three summer months of 1977 for a trip to the west coast. We were getting embarrassed by the number of our European friends who had visited more states in our homeland than we had. Besides, we were eager to take Debbie, who was now nine years old, along with us. The trip was all that we hoped for and more. Following an itinerary suggested by our much traveled friends, Fred and Yoshiko Parkhurst, we drove out by a southern route (walking across the border to Mexico at El Paso) and returned by a northern route (ferrying to Canada at Sault Ste. Marie). Debbie was pleased to meet cousins from both families of grandparents, in Texas, California and Michigan, and fell in love with her great-aunt Marie, Uncle Mort's widow.

That summer also marked the beginning of another epoch for us. After much planning and maneuvering, David and Tanya had built their home on their portion of our lot. Carroll, Jr. and Louise moved at the same time into the basement apartment of our home. They and Debbie would have their privacy and share the upstairs "parlor" if they wished to entertain visitors and needed more room. As a matter of fact, Louise, who had given Debbie lessons, once arranged a little recital for Debbie to perform for her two sets of grandparents on the parlor grand piano.

Carroll and I spent more and more time in the Grandparents' Apartment, where the word processor, television and king-size bed had been moved. Asthma had finally made Carroll, Jr.'s working conditions at the printing company intolerable. His health still permitted him to be the chief caretaker of our house and grounds and it seemed only fair to us that he be reimbursed for that. He also proved to be a caring house-husband while Louise took a part-time position at the local school cafeteria. Now there was almost always a Feagins at home on our wooded lot, dubbed by our neighbors, Pete and Lucretia Moore, the "Feagins Compound." It pleased us to be able to carry on an extended family tradition rarely practiced now in this country.

Guilford College had added a semester in London to its growing Off-Campus Program during the previous year. The program was flourishing under the leadership of Claude Shotts. A remarkable Quaker educator, he had not been ready to retire at sixty-five or seventy and still was not ready even at eighty. During the summer of 1978, Claude, with the assistance of a native German, Ruth Rothe, and the University of Munich Office for International Students, laid the groundwork for a semester in Munich. Carroll and I were to spend the month between our summer program and the fall semester making further necessary arrangements for this. It was patterned after the semester in London, with two main differences: there would be, for our program, a strong emphasis on German culture, including progress in fluency in the language, and our students were to be housed with families, as we had been under the Junior Year in Munich when I studied there. I was happy to have this opportunity to help form permanent ties between Guilford College and Munich.

Carroll soon became just as enthusiastic as I about checking out recommended families and interviewing prospective English speaking natives to teach the appropriate courses not being handled by us. Between the time in August when we saw the summer group off at Orly Airport and the time in September when we returned to Paris to meet the thirty students for the first semester in Munich, we became thoroughly familiar with the public transportation systems of the city, as we visited personally every home to which one or two young persons were assigned. The semester that followed was perhaps the most exciting of any of our years of teaching, and the venture was successful.

* * *

Since 1974, Carroll has increasingly experienced the side effects of lithium—a hand tremor and speech difficulties. I often chided him when he complained of his halting speech: "Oh, you just don't realize that your ready flow of language and almost perfect articulation was a rare gift. Now, for the first time, you are talking like the rest of us. For us, not every word comes out always as intended, as it always has for you. You're just joining the human race!" Fortunately, later on, a substitute for lithium was found that did not have these side-effects.

In 1979, his doctor was so impressed by the fact that there had been no depressions for almost five years that he decided to eliminate the lithium. The result was miraculous. I was as overjoyed as Carroll to watch the slight palsy and quivering lip rapidly and completely disappear. We hoped and prayed that there would be no more cycles of ups and downs.

We began that summer in high spirits. After having had the successful summer and fall-semester programs the year before, we had decided to spend these months at home—particularly because we were trying the experiment with the medication. Carroll had more time for his music and we also saw more of our friends than usual. Everything was wonderful—for several weeks. Then I began to notice that he was becoming more than rejuvenated. He was beginning to behave like a different person. He, who had always been considerate of others, began to think primarily of his own interests. At first, I was dismayed and often angry. Then I became fearful as I noticed more and more his lack of judgment. By fall, he had resumed his daily regimen of lithium. And I was moved to write another poem.

ODE TO LITHIUM

Many thousand milligrams
of you, o wondrous metal—
launched into the bloodstream,
shooting its rapids in
countless corpuscles, bearing
Minerva's powders to erratic
impulses, subduing little
monsters of the mind—
have inflicted some measure of
palsy and halting speech;
but if Ponce de Leon had
sipped a fountain where you
bathed, he might have stopped
the search.
A sudden joy of living
and rejuvenated loins,
at your withdrawal,
underscores the truth:
it takes a taste of Old Age
to savor Youth.

Carroll gradually learned to recognize symptoms of a threatening depression and how to ward it off with a mood elevator. In 1980 he was again in good health and joined me in conducting our last summer school in East/West Germany. His exuberance sparked enthusiasm in all participants.

The situation changed in 1982. Because it was our year of retirement, I was not too surprised when he became intense in everything he was doing in connection with the final semester of teaching. I saw the same upward swing in mood and thoughtlessness that I had become familiar with for the first time during the summer of 1979. Exuberance turned into a relentless drive to get from and give everything that he could to his last semester of students. It was obvious that he was not facing the prospect of retiring as easily as I. After all, I would be returning to a way of life similar to that of our first ten years at Guilford. I was looking forward to staying in the same environment and enjoying the freedom of no fixed schedule. He, on the other hand, was living only for this last semester of teaching. It was almost as if he was involved in a love affair with his last group of students to the point of rejecting any other commitments. He allowed his classes to occupy all of his attention, while he grew more and more impatient with what he called my intrusions into his space. Yet, in most respects, he was performing so well and was meaning so much to his students that I felt compelled to ignore signs of a possible repeat of his first extreme upward swing.

At the commencement exercises, we gave the invocation in the form of a responsive reading that Carroll had prepared. Few present would have surmised the difficulties we two had weathered during the preceding semester. We received the usual expressions of appreciation for long years of service and accepted with gratitude the traditional gift of a captain's or a rocking chair. We chose one of each. The Department of Philosophy celebrated a Carroll Feagins Day and the Department of Foreign Languages gave a party in my honor. Seemingly, this was the beautiful culmination of two teaching careers. Nevertheless, a period of depression for Carroll and frustration for me followed.

Fortunately, our doctor, by now our good friend as well as psychiatrist, was able to guide us through the troubling weeks. He had been present at the evening program to hear Carroll's response to Jimmy Childress, a former student who was already a recognized scholar and professor and had been invited to give the lecture in Carroll's honor. The response had gone well. I was happy that Carroll, Jr. and David were present to share my pride in their father. This made it easier to bear the distress that was coming.

I had adopted a practice that would help me to cope with future mood swings and would keep me from making them worse. When my feelings were most offended, instead of berating him for his behavior, I described it and my own feelings about it in writing. Then, if after reflection I thought it might be good for him to read what I had written, I would share it with him in a quiet moment. During one particular period, I reached a low ebb, where I felt compelled to write a "sermon" to myself. I kept it for future reference and found the DO's easier to follow than the DO NOTs:

DO	DO NOT
Bring up and support subjects of general interest; politics, religion, new building project at New Garden, etc.	Do not express concern about his behavior.
Agree with his expressed opinions when possible; keep silent otherwise.	In general, do not comment on our difficulties together.
Act in a loving, accepting way, even when you don't feel like it.	Do not say anything that resembles preaching or moralizing; refrain from scolding expressions or gestures.
Keep a good sense of humor ready for appropriate expression (be careful of possible misinterpretation of what normally would be appreciated as humor.)	Do not make overtures of an intrusive or forceful kind when he is withdrawing or rejecting.
	Do not reject him even when he has rejected you.

By August after our retirement in May, the doctor considered Carroll's depression sufficiently lifted for us to fly to Kenya for an international conference of the Friends World Committee for Consultation. I trusted that he would again prove correct in his prediction that the trip would do us good.

The long flight to Nairobi was tiring. As usual, I got little sleep but rested in silence while Carroll sat with closed eyes. The plane came down three times, but we were able to de-plane only once, at the airport in Lagos, Nigeria. Carroll's interest in the local scene was aroused sufficiently to alleviate his feelings of apprehension. Besides, he was not the only person who was experiencing anxiety. Before we had left Kennedy Airport, our group had been forewarned of a change in our accommodations in Nairobi because of a military coup that had just taken place. There had been violent activity in the hotel where we had reservations.

Arriving under such conditions was difficult for all of us. We were met by police, who escorted our buses to the assigned hotel. It proved to be both humorous and ironic that military guards watched over our Quaker delegation for our entire stay in Kaimosi. Some of the Quakers did not waste the opportunity to make friends of the military police and soon had them wearing peace emblems on their uniforms.

By the end of the first week, Carroll had recovered and spent a week in Nairobi while I attended the second week of the conference at Kaimosi. Both of us were in excellent spirits by then. On the way back to the States we were able to enjoy stopovers in Munich, Dresden and both Berlins, where we had happy reunions with our German friends without the responsibilities of student programs.

HYMN OF KENYA
(In Quaker Meeting)

Out of the silence
now radiates
the light of music.
vision of swaying voices,
black notes dancing
to rhythmic drum of Kenya.
And remembering again
melodious worship
at Kakamega,
I sing unto the Lord
a new song.

14

STARGATE

1983

For five years after our retirement, Carroll's ups and downs seemed to have settled into a nicely limited span with good balance. Lithium kept him from being quite as creative and exciting as he normally was, but it was wonderful that he was escaping deep depressions. He was feeling so well that he decided to take a solo trip to Georgia in late 1989 to visit old haunts from childhood. He phoned me every night and returned, a day early, in good spirits.

Carroll began playing the piano for "tea and tune time" on Tuesday afternoons in the solarium at Friends Homes, which was to be our future retirement home. He also substituted for New Garden's organist occasionally. After my brother David's death in 1984, I took an orientation course with Hospice and was a volunteer until my seventieth birthday. I wished to show in this way the gratitude I felt for the way Hospice of Baltimore had made David's last months so painless and enriched.

David and Tanya added to our leisure opportunities by building a vacation home called "Stargate" on Emerald Isle on the Outer Banks, north of Jacksonville, North Carolina and giving us a set of keys. We continued to enjoy our "extended family" life on the edge of the campus. Debbie, now a Guilford College student, lived on campus most of the year.

I began seeing more of Ann Deagon after her husband's death in 1986 despite her full schedule of teaching and writing. She kept me in touch with what was going on at Guilford. Carroll and I managed, during stays at Stargate, to finish a group of about thirty Quakerly hymns. He had said all along that if Quakers were going to sing in meetings for worship, they should quit singing mostly typical Protestant hymns. He composed some and adapted other appropriate music, and I wrote most of the words, some of which we hoped would be included in a songbook. The meeting began using some of the songs almost immediately with good response.

Around this time, we had a visit from Jillian Haeseler and her husband, Miguel Lechuga. Jillian had been a German major at Guilford. I like to think of her as my academic daughter, the offspring of my deepest desire as a teacher—to share the joy of learning in the classroom. She recognized this desire and met it with enthusiasm. Furthermore, she successfully completed her Junior Year in Munich and, in Heidelberg, earned a new degree in teaching German as a second language.

She was in Munich to greet us with our students during two of our stays there and helped introduce them to this favorite city. She also pursued and eventually earned a doctorate in languages. She was living with her husband and their daughter Lorca in Madrid, where she was Director of the Department of English and Communications for Saint Louis University in Spain.

This was their first visit with us since a brief stop over on their honeymoon. It brought us a taste of youthful happiness, hope and cheer at a time of depression. Since then, she has sent us a copy of her recently published intermediate textbook for German and continues to make me proud that she was my student.

Our granddaughter is married to a recent graduate of North Carolina State University, Nizam Yousef. I enjoy watching him introduce her to another culture, as he learns more about ours through her. I can only watch them from a distance, however. Even though the Hilty and Feagins grandparents want to help smooth their pathway when they have difficulties, we know that all children ultimately must make their own way. They seem to have made a good start. I have given them a copy of this poem.

SPECTRUM

for Debbie and Nizam
Allah by name, in sheer unprismed light,
the silence breaking: "Long ago you knew,

Confucius, of the golden rule; and you,
Siddhartha, of the eightfold path of right
causing Ashoka to convert his sword
into pillars of peace; and you, my Son,
have lived as I would have my will be done
and died a sacrifice, with love restored.
As Krishna promised, I assume on earth
new forms to serve new ages in distress.
How long before our followers confess
their kinship over accident of birth?
"Each shares the Light along the prism's scale;
without each one, refracted light would pale."

Carroll and I celebrated our fiftieth wedding anniversary alone at
Stargate. He was recovering from a shoulder-joint replacement. I
feared that another cloud of depression was descending upon him af-
ter a summer upswing that I had scarcely been able to keep up with.
Still, the summer had been fun. We visited several friends whom we
expected not to see again and attended the Feagins family reunion at
Feagins Gap near Kingsport, Tennessee. We celebrated again on
Emerald Isle.

We toasted each other in tiny Ettaler goblets, gifts of Karl
Fischer, with Ettaler bitters, which I had saved secretly from our trip
to the cloister in 1980. We photographed ourselves at the Point of
Emerald Isle, by my making a dash from the camera to the pavilion
bench, and then in the living room at Stargate.

We have a lot to celebrate, Carroll and I. It occurs to me that I
have used many words to describe what happens when we are "out of
balance." I have not said enough about the good times. How many
times Carroll has awakened me at Stargate by playing the Aeolian
console piano, which fits the niche at the top of the stairs in David's
and Tanya's house. There we have enjoyed walks on the beach, especially the walk that was accompanied by a school of dolphins performing their graceful arcs for a quarter of a mile to the inlet, where
they left us to turn out to sea.

I cannot mention Carroll's playing for me at Stargate without
remembering his playing for countless others, especially the attenders of New Garden Meeting, who recognized his unique touch and
expression. I have often wondered how far he could have gone if he
had chosen music instead of teaching as his vocation. But, then, his
students would have missed the benefits of an especially gifted

teacher if he had not pursued his love of philosophy and adopted the Socratic way of sharing the search for truth.

I have failed, perhaps, to express my gratitude for the chance to live so closely with Carroll. If this begins to sound like a memorial or a eulogy, it is for the reason that there are times, during his periods of depression, when I felt what seemed like the grief of a widow and mourned the person who was "absent" (or wished to be). Why is it that we have to lose, or almost lose, what is precious to us before we express our appreciation?

MY SONG WHEN YOU ARE ILL

What sly invader creeps
into well ordered woods
overwhelming the custodian,
stalks the gentle beasts,
disorients the footless ones
and from fragile receptacles
strips the delicate calyces
shattering petals
into muddied pools?

Unbind, O strange one,
the custodian
to attend the blossoms,
restore music to the forests!
Unstartle the pennant-winged
that their fluttering may soar
with direction once more and return
with nourishment to the nests.

Anxiety lurks mind caverns
ticking their secret time.
Compassion waits outside the park
with frightened eyes.

I am approaching, I feel rather sure, a good stopping point in my story. But before I continue, I must write briefly about the death of Polly Cobb in October 1989. Whit has written a beautiful memorial, filed among papers I cherish. This will be a "memory" of our last visit together at Stargate.

We were on top-deck, above the yaupon, pine and oak, which are intertwined with wild grapevines. Although at a dizzying height, we felt secure with the deck's firm railings and attachments to the roof. Being so close to the Point, we had views of the ocean in two directions and across the sandbars of the inlet to small islands. We had glimpses of the Intracoastal Waterway beyond.

I cannot remember which of us called attention to seven (or thirteen? or more?) pelicans flying in graceful, V-shaped formation. I tried to count them, but Polly was speaking. "I love it up here. The view is always lovely and always changing. The late autumn's sun is easier to take than the summer's. Even under a hot sun, there is usually a cool breeze. I love the coast almost as much as the mountains."

We often commented on our preferences for the mountains or the coast and never failed to express appreciation for the top-deck and its views. On this particular day, I remember, we moved soon to a lower deck, where I read relevant portions of my book aloud to Polly. Suddenly she burst into tears over the account of the accidental deaths of our mutual friends, David and Cora Worth Parsons. I, too, felt this sadness as I realized that they had never seen their grandchildren. Our expressions of sorrow led to exchanges of confidences about our recent experiences and relationships. Polly was especially understanding of me. Her sense of humor was remarkable for one who had to put up with health problems as she did. She let nothing interfere for long with her passion for learning and teaching.

Polly's death was widely mourned and especially felt in the city of Blacksburg, Virginia. I feel blessed to have shared so many happy times with her since the years when our families lived side by side on the edge of the Guilford College campus. I miss her still, as I turn to other close friends in addition to Ed, who has always been there for both Carroll and me; to Whit; to our neighbors, Lucretia and "Pete" Moore; to Debbie's other grandparents, Janet and Hiram Hilty; and to Ann Deagon, especially. Three professional nurses, Pat, Chris and Gracia, have made my recent years happier and more meaningful in various ways by their acts of loving kindness. Every weekday has been enriched by the habit of spending a relaxing hour with Maxine Ljung, longtime friend, before going to dinner at Friends Homes.

* * *

There has been another death, this one in my family, which has deeply affected me. It is that of Mike, the younger son of my brother Joe and his wife Delma. The only one of their four children not to marry, he had remained close to the family and was present and a source of joy for reunions of any kind. Late in July 1987, Joe phoned telling of Mike's having been diagnosed with AIDS.

After Mike's death, November 30, 1989, Delma assembled over twenty pages of her writing describing the many aspects of their family's ordeal with the frightful disease. I have these pages before me and wish they could be published for all to read. The tribute she pays to the last doctor to treat Mike speaks for the dedication of some caring doctors who may go unrecognized.

* * *

I always think of our own doctors when I reread Delma's words. Without the faithful family doctor and our psychiatrist, Carroll and I could not have coped as well as we have. We have been experiencing the longest period of depression ever. It began soon after our fiftieth wedding anniversary. Carroll has spent so many weeks in Cone Hospital that, for one "benefit" period, we have had to use all but fifteen of his sixty lifetime reserve days covered by Medicare. Without Medicare and our AAUP insurance supplement, we would be financially bankrupt. But we do have them, fortunately, and need worry only about a possible bankruptcy of my spirit of optimism.

Living with a depression is quite different from living through the periods of self-centered euphoria that characterize the upswings. I can scarcely recall how desperate and helpless I felt during those times. All I can say is that, at times, the situation was so bad that either Carroll had to leave for a visit with Ed until he was hospitalized or I had to spend a few days of "R and R" with Ann until lithium had brought Carroll to his usual thoughtful self. It is my hope that the slowness with which he is coming out of this depression may mean that it will be his last and that he will never again swing too far upward. It is a real possibility, for his upswings seemed to be getting briefer.

* * *

Humor is the saving virtue for coping with our problems. I have tried to nourish any sense of humor I may have been born with. Carroll has normally had a better one. Two poems illustrate how expressing myself in this way has helped me to recover myself:

PORCUPINES

How like a porcupine
our love lately
frustrating flaws of
character long familiar
taken comfortably for granted
are sharper than ever
mutually destructive
driving us apart.

Out of our caring
each approaching the other
for the usual warmth
of touching and sharing
suddenly the old
quills
!!!

INDIGNITY

Give me back my queen!
Toppled
she lies again
beneath attack.
Your maneuver earned a
pawn perhaps
but not a queen.

I view the field
am tempted to retreat
cease playing forever
the game. If only you
could feel my defeat and
make the reconciling move
you so disarming might know:
Without arms one cannot be
expected to embrace.

I have resorted to fantasy, too, as therapy. As this depression
dragged on and I began to look forward, more and more, to office

visits, I grew aware of how emotionally dependent on our psychiatrist I was becoming. Finding it difficult to deal with this, I thought of a way to communicate my problem to him by writing a series of poems expressing some rather complex feelings. I "made a fool of myself" and called her Alice. "Apollo" best represents Carroll for me, and who better than Asclepius for the doctor? These poems, delivered, one by one, during office visits, are an important part of my healing:

TRANSFERENCE?

Lewis Carroll's cat
lingered long
in a haunting grin.
You, avatar of Asclepius,
sparkled in eyes of healing love
spiced with humor
and, with no apparent malice
captivated Alice.

THE DOCTOR

Briefly with her alone,
this gentle friend
holds her restless hands
quietly in his own,
feeding her passion peace
with healing art,
understands and tames
the tiger of her heart.

Caring compassion makes
her darkness bright;
she regains her self
in love sustained by light.

TO ASCLEPIUS

For her, poetry
has served as a fence
guarding fantasies and impulses
keeping her in your presence
from being too tearful.
For you? Perhaps a defense,
a reminder: be no kinder to her
than you are. Of one starved
for such caring you may well
be careful.

EXCUSES TO ASCLEPIUS

Alice is a part of me
that comes alive
whenever you are near;
always young and eager to communicate,
she gropes for words but then
suppresses them.
What can she say at all appropriate
for my years?

The Cheshire has her tongue
and grins from ear to ear
because it knows that Alice
still belongs to Wonderland
while I belong to here and now
with over twenty years between.

What can I do, my dear Asclepius?
Alice finds your medicine so sweet,
your manner of healing so appealing,
she pulls me through the glass of time.

THE ETHICAL QUESTION

What right have I
to thwart his will to die?
Though I still see in him the young Apollo
still feel his light, still listen
for his music and know that there is more,
if he would put aside a mask grown heavy,
lay down the instrument he tires of playing,
how can I ask for what was never mine?

I do possess shared hopes and memories
of good things realized, should be content
to let him go to breathe the air of Socrates,
his kindred soul. But then I count
the empty hours in store for me and cry,
"Eternity can wait; please, stay with me!"

It hurts to think he finds in life such pain,
he would forsake our dear Asclepius
for Dr. Death.

MY HYMN TO APOLLO

They dubbed you Plato
long ago, I know,
and it suited you,
Professor of Philosophy.
But you are my Apollo,
Source of light and music;
it's what you'll always be
to me.
Apollo is supposed
to rise and paint
the skies, not lie in bed
till noon, hiding
his light under the covers
and saying, "I can't get up
today," Get up, my sleepyhead,
and soon!

The night has been too long
filled with darkness
without rest,
nightmares without dreams.
Let morning once again
be blessed with your music;
let your light appear
on my horizon!

PATIENCE ON A PLATEAU

"We are waiting,"
he said to Apollo. "for
your return."

"We are waiting together,"
she sang to herself, knowing
from the start they would
have to be apart.

Waiting for Apollo
even with Asclepius
is long—it means
waiting on, too,
sometimes serving
unwillingly
and with divided
heart.

It might be easier
if she would stay away
from mirrors. Her aging
is daily more perceptible
than Apollo's progress
—so very slow—
seen only by looking back
at past plateaus.
But Alice is drawn
to looking-glasses
and she could die
of patience.

Alice gradually slipped away from me and back into Wonderland. The doctor's frequently repeated promise that Carroll would
come out of this long depression appeared to be coming true. Added
to the words of promise, however, was his suggestion that life might
prove easier for us if we moved sooner to Friends Homes than we had
planned. We decided now to do so. Our extended family would be extended hardly any further at all, for we did not have to sell our home,
and our sons and their wives remain in their two adjacent houses on
Nathan Hunt Road on the other side of Guilford College campus.

ABOVE: *Carroll, Jr. and I with my parents after leaving Sullins College (1944).*

BELOW: *Andjelko Eskic between David and Carroll, Jr. before our home on Nathan Hunt Road, Guilford College.*

ABOVE: *Disembarking at Santorini during tour of Greek Isles with Whit and Polly Cobb. (Whit in center of photo).* BELOW: *Portrait in India. Standing: Jack Sutters, Carroll and our son David. Office Secretary (seated) soon to be married under "favorable signs" respecting wishes of her grandfather.*

Photo taken by Carroll at entrance of Baptist Church in Moscow with our hostess for the service and a lunch afterwards. Here is where he was spontaneously asked to play the organ prelude (1971). [Nixon posed in the same spot for the news a year later.]

Offices of American Friends Service Committee and Friends Service Council of London were located in this building. Worship and other meetings were held here.

Arjan Das, the "Hindu Quaker" ("Quindu"), abiding spirit of Quaker House in New Delhi.

ABOVE: *Carroll, Jr. at home on Nathan Hunt Road.*

RIGHT: *Louise with Debbie while she and Carroll, Jr. were house-sitting for Ed Burrows during his year of travel.*

David and Tanya, both public-school principals, chaperoning high school prom.

Carroll and Mary with Jillian Haeseler.

Nizam Yousef and Debbie in Raleigh, North Carolina public park.

Ann Deagon helping me prepare my art show at Friends Homes.

Carroll playing organ in Hobbs Hall, Friends Homes.

EPILOGUE
1999

In April 1995, Carroll and I moved to Friends Homes, across from Guilford College campus on New Garden Road. We are within walking distance of New Garden Friends Meeting. Since we have moved to Friends Homes our lives have been enriched by closer contacts with old and new friends. We continue to have all the privacy we need when we want it. Along with this comes the chance to do things we have never had time for before. I even had my first art show here, of paintings and poems. Important for me, also, is the time I can reserve for reflection and writing. The gift of an organ to Hobbs Hall has helped to lift Carroll's depression. Perhaps my happiest hours are spent listening to his playing three mornings weekly for music lovers like me.

It suddenly occurs to me that the word "becoming" in the title of my book might have a counterpart: "begoing." Carroll celebrated his eighty-second birthday in July and I'll be eighty-two in November. Have we not done most of our becoming by this time? From now on, will it be begoing, begoing? As a Hospice volunteer, I learned a valuable lesson from the dying: for many, growth and enrichment can continue to be experienced to the end. Then, there is the word "begone"! I'll address it to any gloomy line of thought that might follow here and turn my attention to more positive thinking, satisfied that "becoming" need not have a negative counterpart and can remain the only relevant verb linking my present and future.

Becoming myself, I have come to realize, is a complex process. I am using the word "becoming" as a verb, of course, although as an adjective it evokes interesting ideas: "tending to suit or to give a pleasing effect . . . , as to a person or thing." I like the Aristotelian definition of the verb form, "to become": "any change involving realization of potentialities, as a movement from the lower level of potentiality to the higher level of actuality." That is what I have always wanted and still want myself to do. Becoming oneself implies a division of selves to start with—whether there be only two, like Goethe's two souls, or many, like Hesse's multiple egos in *Steppenwolf.*

When the Greeks said, "Know thyself!" they really could have meant "Get acquainted with all the aspects of your selves and integrate them if you ever expect to become the self that is potentially yours." I am sure this need not involve imaginary selves, like Alice. I knew I was making her up and that I allowed her to be what I did not want any of my real selves to be. My androgynous self, appearing in sculpture and poem, was different; it remained dormant for years, waiting for another such self to appear and throw some light on the shadowy boundaries. When this did happen, for a brief interlude, it was not too difficult for this self to be reintegrated happily within my whole being.

I should also point out that the Inner Companion mentioned in my story is not one of my selves. It is the integrating force, I believe, of my conflicting selves. I could comfortably call it God, or, in the concept of the late Algie Newlin, my Mystic Confidant[e], whom I call upon for guidance and courage. No matter where I am or what is happening, this spiritual part of my being is present whenever I seek it. I am grateful for its comforting effect and expect to have its illuminating presence with me forever.

THE PERFECT IS REALLY FUTURE

I am
what I am
this is my time and place
these my friends   these my circumstances
serving my ends   my destiny   now
taking chances   while my angle bends
fortuitously   to the unique modulation
of my frequency   the single codification
of my pattern   my genetic formulation
DNA/RNA   as my case may be   I am
in time and place with other
entia   varied coded patterns dotting
space   all rays of life   "sent on"   (to
quote Buckminster Fuller)   "from a remote
source"   integrities that interact   are
free   for transforming   embracing   displacing
or even exploding an accomplished "coding"
yet   every living order leaves its trace
so I   for my brief crossing of
place with time   among the many   am one
the fact of my becoming is never in future
undone: the tense   "I shall have been"
the statement of Me   stays   to haunt the
face of time and space
forever